T0324338

The Traveler, the Tower, and the Worm

MATERIAL TEXTS

ALBERTO MANGUEL

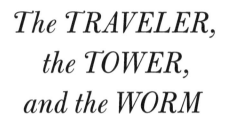

The TRAVELER, the TOWER, and the WORM

The Reader as Metaphor

UNIVERSITY OF PENNSYLVANIA PRESS

PHILADELPHIA

Published by
University of Pennsylvania Press
Philadelphia, Pennsylvania 19104-4112
www.upenn.edu/pennpress

Printed in the United States of America on acid-free paper
10 9 8 7 6 5 4 3 2 1

Library of Congress Cataloging-in-Publication Data
Manguel, Alberto.
The traveler, the tower, and the worm : the reader as metaphor / Alberto Manguel.
1st ed.
p. cm. (Material texts)
Includes bibliographical references and index.
ISBN: 978-0-8122-4523-3 (hardcover : alk. paper)
1. Literature and anthropology. 2. Literature and society.
3. Signs and symbols. 4. Books and reading—Philosophy.
GN452.5.M36 2013   2013005806
809.3   dc23

For Craig, with all my love

CONTENTS

INTRODUCTION

> There are no such things as facts, only interpretation.
> —Friedrich Nietzsche, *Posthumous Papers*

As far as we can tell, we are the only species for whom the world seems to be made of stories. Biologically developed to be conscious of our existence, we treat our perceived identities and the identity of the world around us as if they required a literate decipherment, as if everything in the universe were represented in a code that we are supposed to learn and understand. Human societies are based on this assumption: that we are, up to a point, capable of understanding the world in which we live.

To understand the world, or to try and understand it, translation of experience into language is not enough. Language barely glances the surface of our experience, and transmits from one person to another, in a supposedly shared conventional code, imperfect and ambiguous notations that rely both on the careful intelligence of the one who speaks or writes and

Hildegard von Bingen, "Cosmic Man."
From *Liber divinorum operum* (c. 1170–1174).

on the creative intelligence of the one who listens or reads. To enhance the possibilities of mutual understanding and to create a larger space of meaning, language resorts to metaphors that are, ultimately, a confession of language's failure to communicate directly. Through metaphors, experiences in one field become illuminated by experiences in another.

Aristotle suggested that the power of a metaphor resides in the recognition conjured up in the audience;[1] that is to say, the audience must invest the subject of the metaphor with a particular shared meaning. Literate societies, societies based on the written word, have developed a central metaphor to name the perceived relationship between human beings and their universe: the world as a book that we are meant to read. The ways in which this reading is conducted are many—through fiction, mathematics, cartography, biology, geology, poetry, theology, and myriad other forms—but their basic assumption is the same: that the universe is a coherent system of signs governed by specific laws, and that those signs have a meaning, even if that meaning lies beyond our grasp. And that in order to glimpse that meaning, we try to read the book of the world.

Not every literate society assumes this central image in the same way, and the different vocabularies that we have developed to name the act of reading reflect, at specific times and in specific places, the ways in which a certain society defines its own identity. Cicero, contesting Aristotle's assumptions, warned against the idle use of metaphors merely for adornment's sake. In *On Oratory*, he wrote that "just as clothes were in the beginning invented to protect us against the cold and later began to be worn as adornment and dignity, the use of metaphors started because of poverty but became of common use for the sake of entertainment."[2] For Cicero, metaphors are born from the poverty of language, that is to say, from the inability of words to name our experience exactly and concretely. To use metaphors in a merely decorative function is to debase their essential enriching power.

Out of a basic identifying metaphor society develops a chain of metaphors. The world as book links to life as a voyage, and so the reader is seen as a traveler, advancing through the pages of that book. Sometimes, however, on that journey the traveler does not engage with the landscape and its inhabitants but proceeds, as it were, from sanctuary to sanctuary; the activity of reading is then confined to a space in which the traveler withdraws from the world instead of living in the world. The biblical metaphor of the tower denoting purity and virginity, applied to the Bride in the *Song of Songs* and to the Virgin Mary in medieval iconography, becomes transformed centuries later into the ivory tower of the reader, with its negative connotations of inaction and disinterest in social matters, the opposite of the reader-traveler. The traveler metaphor evolves and the textual pilgrim becomes in the end, like all mortal beings, prey of the Worm of Death, a grandiose image of that other, more modest pest that gnaws through the pages of books, devouring paper and ink. The metaphor folds back upon itself, and just as the

Worm devours the reader-traveler, the reader-traveler (sometimes) devours books, not to benefit from the learning they contain (and life displays) but merely to become bloated with words, reflecting back the work of Death. Thus the reader is derided for being a worm, a mouse, a rat, a creature for whom books (and life) are not nourishment but fodder.

These metaphors are not always explicitly set out. Sometimes the idea presents itself, implicit in its context, but the metaphor that will illuminate it has itself not yet been named. In fact, in some cases, as in that of the ivory tower, the metaphor is created long after the idea has been present in society. It is difficult, except in a few cases, to track the appearance of the metaphors themselves; perhaps more useful, more revealing, is to discuss certain instances of the presence and development of the notion behind the metaphor. In one of my early books, *A History of Reading*, I dedicated several pages to explore the metaphors related to our craft. I attempted to trace some of the most common ones but felt that the subject merited a more in-depth exploration; the result of that insatisfaction is the present book.

Readers of the printed word are constantly being told that their tools are old-fashioned, their methods outmoded, that they must learn the new technologies or be left behind by the galloping herd. Perhaps. But if we are gregarious animals who must follow the dictates of society, we are nevertheless individuals who learn about the world by reimagining it, by putting words to it, by reenacting through those words our experience.

In the end, it may be more interesting, more illuminating to concentrate on that which does not change in our craft, on that which radically defines the act of reading, on the vocabulary we use to try to understand, as self-conscious beings, this unique ability born from the need to survive through imagination and through hope.

CHAPTER 1

THE READER AS TRAVELER

Reading as Recognition of the World

You will not discover the limits of the soul
by traveling, even if you wander over every
conceivable path, so deep is its story.

—Heraclitus, fragment 35

The Book of the World

> To lay before you the marvellous book of the entire
> universe, and have you read the excellence of its
> Author in the living letters of its creatures.
> —Luis de Granada, *The Symbol of Faith*

In the left margin of a fifteenth-century French manuscript,[1] a
small illumination serves as incipit for the text. It shows, against
a dark blue sky studded with golden stars, a woman looking

upon a baby child strapped to its cradle. The scene depicted is Moses in the bulrushes. The woman is Miriam, Moses's sister, who convinces the Pharaoh's daughter to have the child Moses nursed by a Jewish nurse; unbeknownst to the princess, the nurse is Jochebed, Moses's mother. The child in the illumination is Moses himself; the basket in which he is sent downriver is a thick, red, bound book. In an effort to ally the teachings of the New Testament with those of the Old, medieval commentators traced parallels between the two, providing artists and sermonists with a rich iconography. The Virgin Mary mirrored Moses's mother, who regained her youth after her hundred and fifty-sixth year and married her husband Amram a second time: Mary's virginity was read as equivalent to Jochebed's new virginal state. Like the angel who announced to Mary the birth of Christ, God told Amram that his wife would bear a child whose memory "would be celebrated while the world lasts, and not only among the Hebrews, but among strangers also." To escape the Pharaoh's edict that decreed the slaughter of all Hebrew male children (as Herod would later, in Mary's time), Jochebed made a cradle out of bulrushes, daubed it with pitch on the outside, and abandoned it on the shores of the Red Sea.[2] The image is taken up in the exquisite illumination, combining in one depiction the reenactment of the scene in Exodus, Miriam watching over the child Moses as Mary will later watch

Moses in a book, *Grandes Heures de Rohan* (c. 1430–1435).
Courtesy the Bibliothèque nationale de France.

over the infant Jesus, and the promise that the Book will carry Moses into the world, implicitly announcing the coming of the Savior. The Book is the vessel that allows the word of God to travel through the world, and those readers who follow it become pilgrims in the deepest, truest sense.

The book is many things. As a repository of memory, a means of overcoming the constraints of time and space, a site for reflection and creativity, an archive of the experience of ourselves and others, a source of illumination, happiness, and sometimes consolation, a chronicle of events past, present, and future, a mirror, a companion, a teacher, a conjuring-up of the dead, an amusement, the book in its many incarnations, from clay tablet to electronic page, has long served as a metaphor for many of our essential concepts and undertakings. Almost since the invention of writing, more than five thousand years ago, the signs that stood for words that expressed (or attempted to express) our thinking appeared to its users as models or images for things as intricate and aimless, as concrete or as abstract as the world in which we live and even life itself. Very quickly, the first scribes must have realized the magical properties of their new craft. For those who had mastered its code, the art of writing allowed the faithful transmission of lengthy texts so that the messenger had no longer to rely solely on his or her memory; it lent authority to the text set down, perhaps for no other reason than that its material existence now offered the spoken word a tangible reality—and, at the same time, by manipulating that assumption, allowed for this authority to be distorted or undermined; it helped organize and render coherent intricacies of reasoning that often became lost in speech, whether in convolutions of monologues or in the ramifications of dialogue. Perhaps we cannot imagine today what it must have felt like for people accustomed to requiring the bodily presence of a live speaker to suddenly receive, in a clump of clay, the voice of a distant friend or a long dead king. It is not surprising that such a miraculous instrument should appear in the mind of these early readers as the metaphorical manifestation of other miracles, of the inconceivable universe, and of their unintelligible lives.

The remnants of Mesopotamian literature bear witness to both the sense of marvel of the scribes and the extraordinary uses to which the new craft was put. For example, in *The Epic of Enmerkar and the Lord of Aratta*, composed sometime in the twenty-first century B.C.E., the poet explains that writing was invented as a means of properly conveying a text of many words. "Because the mouth of the messenger was too full, and he was therefore unable to deliver the message, Enmerkar molded a piece of clay and fixed the words upon it. Before that day, it had not been possible for words to cleave to clay." This capacious quality was complemented by that of trustworthiness, as affirmed by the author of a hymn in the twentieth century B.C.E.: "I am a meticulous scribe who leaves nothing out," he assures his readers, heralding the future promises of journalists and historians. At the same time, the possibility of manipulating this same trustworthiness is attested by another scribe, serving under the Akkadian king Ashurbanipal, in the seventh century

B.C.E.: "Everything that will not please the king, I shall delete," the loyal subject declares with disarming frankness.[3]

All these complex characteristics that allowed a written text to reproduce, in the reader's eye, the experience of the world, led to the container of the text (the tablet, later the scroll and the codex) being seen as the world itself. The natural human propensity to find in our physical surroundings a sense, a coherence, a narrative, whether through a system of natural laws or through imagined stories, helped translate the vocabulary of the book into a material one, granting God the art that the gods had bestowed upon humankind: the art of writing. Mountains and valleys became part of a divine language that we were meant to unravel, seas and rivers carried a message from the Creator and, as Plotinus taught in the third century, "if we look at the stars as if they were letters, we can, if we know how to decipher this kind of writing, read the future in their configurations."[4] The creation of a text on a blank page was assimilated to the creation of the universe in the void, and when Saint John stated in his Gospel that "in the beginning was the Word" he was defining as much his own scribal task as that of the Author Himself. By the seventeenth century, the tropes of God as author and the world as book had become so engrained in the Western imagination that they could be once more taken up and rephrased. In *Religio Medici*, Sir Thomas Browne made the now commonplace images his own: "Thus there are two books from whence I collect my Divinity. Besides that written one of God, another of his servant Nature, that universal and publik Manuscript, that lies expans'd unto the eyes of all; those that never saw him in the one, have discovered him in the other."[5]

Though its sources are Mesopotamian, the precise metaphor relating word to world was fixed, in the Jewish tradition, around the sixth century B.C.E. The ancient Jews, lacking for the most part a vocabulary to express abstract ideas, often preferred to use concrete nouns as metaphors for those ideas rather than inventing new words for new concepts, thereby lending these nouns a moral and spiritual meaning.[6] Thus, for the complex idea of living consciously in the world and attempting to draw from the world its God-given meaning, they borrowed the image of the volume that held God's word, the Bible or "the Books." And for the bewildering realization of being alive, of life itself, they chose an image used for describing the act of reading these books: the image of the traveled road.[7] Both metaphors—book and road—have the advantage of great simplicity and popular awareness, and the passage from the image to the idea (or, as my old schoolbook would say, from the *vehicle* to the *tenor*)[8] can be smoothly and naturally effected. To live, then, is to travel through the book of the world, and to read, to make one's way through a book, is to live, to travel through the world itself. An oral communication exists almost exclusively in the present of the listener; a written text occupies the full extension of the reader's time. It extends *visibly* into the past of pages already read and into the future of those to come, much as we can see the road already traveled and intuit the one waiting before us, much as we know that a number of years lie behind us and

(though there is no assurance of this) that a number of years lie ahead. Listening is largely a passive endeavor; reading is an active one, like traveling. Contrary to later perceptions of the act of reading that opposed it to that of acting in the world, in the Judeo-Christian tradition words read elicited action: "Write

St. John devouring a book. Jean Duvet, *The Apocalypse* (1561).
© Trustees of the British Museum.

the vision," says God to the prophet Habakkuk, "and make it plain upon tables, that he may run who readeth it."[9]

Composed probably a century after the prophecies of Habakkuk, the Book of Ezekiel offers an even clearer metaphor of the readable world. In a vision, Ezekiel sees the heavens open and a hand appear, holding a scroll of parchment that is then spread before him, "written within and without; and there was written therein lamentations, and mourning, and woe."[10] This scroll the prophet must eat so that he may speak the ingested words to the children of Israel. Much the same image is later taken up by Saint John on Patmos. In his Book of Revelation, an angel descends from Heaven with an open volume. "Take it and eat it up," says the angel, "and it shall make thy belly bitter, but it shall be in thy mouth sweet as honey."[11]

Both Ezekiel and John's images gave rise to an extensive library of biblical commentaries that, throughout the Middle Ages and the Renaissance, see in this double book an image of God's double creation, the Book of Scripture and the Book of Nature, both of which we are meant to read and in which we are written. Talmudic commentators associated the double book with the double tablets of the Torah. According to Midrash, the Torah that God gave Moses on Mount Sinai was both a written text and an oral commentary. During the day, when it was light, Moses read the text God had written on the tablets; in the darkness of the night he studied the commentary God had spoken when he created the world.[12] For the Talmudists, the Book of Nature is understood as God's oral gloss on his own written text. Perhaps for this reason Philo de Biblos, in the second century, declared that the Egyptian god Thoth had invented simultaneously the art of writing and that of composing commentaries or glosses.[13]

For Saint Bonaventure, in the thirteenth century, Ezekiel's book is both the word and the world. God, says Bonaventure, "created this perceptible world as a means of self-revelation so that, like a mirror of God or a divine footprint, it might lead man to love and praise his Creator. Accordingly, there are two books, one written within, and that is [inscribed by] God's eternal Art and Wisdom; the other written without, and that is the perceptible world."[14] Faced with God's double creation, we are entrusted with the role of readers, to follow God's text and to interpret it to the best of our abilities. For Bonaventure, the constant temptation, the true *demonic* temptation, is expressed in the words of the serpent to Eve in the Garden: "Ye shall be as gods."[15] That is to say, instead of wishing to serve the Word of God as readers, we want to be like God himself, the author of our own book.[16]

Saint Augustine made this explicit in his *Confessions*, using his own childhood experience as example. How is it, he asks, that reading "the fancies dreamed up by poets" may entice us with what is untrue and steer us away from the truth of God? The craft of reading and writing "are by far the better study," but they may lead us to believe in these "hollow fancies."[17] Human beings, according to Augustine, strictly "obey the rules of grammar which have been handed down to them, and yet ignore the eternal rules of everlasting salvation which they have received" from God himself. Our task therefore consists in balancing the experience of the pleasurable illusions created by the poets' words, with the knowledge that they *are* illusions; to enjoy the translation into words of that which can be felt and known on this earth, and, at the same time, to distance ourselves from that knowledge and that feeling in order to read more clearly the contents of God's word as written in his books. Augustine distinguishes between reading what is false and reading what is true. For Augustine, the experience of reading Virgil, for example, carries all the material problems that the reading of the sacred texts does, and one of the questions to be resolved is the degree of importance a reader is permitted to attach to either. "I was obliged to memorize the wanderings of a hero named Aeneas," writes Augustine, "while in the meantime I failed to remember my own erratic ways. I learned to lament the death of Dido, who killed herself for love, while all the time, in the midst of these things, I was dying, separated from you, my God and my Life, and I shed no tears for my own plight."[18] The physical literary road taken by Aeneas becomes Augustine's own mistaken metaphorical road of life, while the book in which he reads of it can be (but fails to be) a mirror of his own called-for regret.

Reading the Bible has the same metaphorical function. "Between the paths of the Bible and those of its readers," wrote the twentieth-century Israeli novelist Yehuda Amichai, "the words of Scripture are the space that must first be crossed:

the first pilgrimage is that of reading."[19] The Bible is a book of roads and pilgrimages: the departure from Eden, Exodus, the travels of Abraham and of Jacob. In the penultimate chapter of the Pentateuch the last word is "to ascend," that is to say, to travel on, toward the earthly Jerusalem or toward that other, celestial city. To walk, to wander, to saunter (from the Old French "Sainct'Terre," the Holy Land)[20] is to make active use of the Bible's words, just as to read is to travel. This analogy is made explicit in depictions of readers who turn the words on the page into worldly action, from Saint Anthony (who took the words in Matthew 19 literally and went out into the desert with nothing but the Gospel's words)[21] and the prophet Amos (who "reads" his own visions to the people of Israel)[22] to Bunyan's Pilgrim dreaming of a man "turned away from his own house, a book in his hand, and a great burden on his back."[23] We advance through a text as we advance through the world, passing from the first page to the last through the unfolding landscape, sometimes starting in mid-chapter, sometimes not reaching the end. The intellectual experience of crossing the pages as we read becomes a physical experience, calling into action the entire body: hands turning the pages or fingers scrolling the text, legs lending support to the receptive body, eyes scanning for meaning, ears tuned to the sound of the words in our head. The pages to come promise a point of arrival, a glimmer on the horizon; the pages already read allow for the possibility of recollection. And in the present of the text we exist suspended in a constantly changing moment, an island of time shimmer-

ing between what we know of the text and what yet lies ahead. Every reader is an armchair Crusoe.

This becomes apparent in Augustine's understanding of the relationship between the act of reading and the all-too-swift passing through life. "Suppose that I am going to recite a psalm I know," he suggests in the *Confessions*.

> Before I begin, my faculty of expectation is engaged by the whole of it. But once I have begun, as much of the psalm as I have

William Blake, "Christian Reading in His Book."
From Blake's illustrations for John Bunyan's *The Pilgrim's Progress* (c. 1824).

THE READER AS TRAVELER

removed from the province of my expectation and relegated to the past, now engages my memory, and the scope of the action which I am performing is divided between the two faculties of memory and expectation, the one looking back to the part which I have already recited, the other looking forward to the part which I have still to recite. But my faculty of attention is present all the while, and through it passes what was the future in the process of becoming the past. As the process continues, the province of memory is extended in proportion as that of expectation is reduced, until the whole of my expectation is absorbed. This happens when I have finished my recitation and it has passed into the province of memory.

For Augustine, the act of reading is a journey through the text being read, claiming for the province of memory the territory explored, while, in the process, the uncharted landscape ahead gradually diminishes and becomes familiar territory. "What is true of the whole psalm," Augustine continues, "is also true of all its parts and of each syllable. It is true of any longer action in which I may be engaged and of which the recitation of the psalm may only be a small part. It is true of a man's whole life, of which all his actions are parts. It is true of the whole history of humankind, of which each life is a part."[24] The experience of reading and the experience of journeying through life mirror one another.

Traveling Through the Text

In time he recognized the story of this loss
As the end of his journey.

— The Epic of Gilgamesh

By the time Augustine was writing his *Confessions*, the idea of the reader as traveler was already ancient. Though Augustine could not have known it, the traveling reader appears in one of our oldest narratives, the *Epic of Gilgamesh*, first written around 1750 B.C.E. and refined and reassembled some two centuries later. The revised composition, known as the "Ninevite version," was found inscribed on eleven clay tablets.[25] In the first verses of the first tablet, the poet presents his hero, the great king Gilgamesh, and the marvel he built, the fortified city of Uruk. And then the poet addresses the reader:

> Look at these walls, tight as a net for birds!
> Consider their base, how incomparable!

Jadeite cylinder seal showing Gilgamesh fighting a lion (Akkadian period, c. 2350–2150 B.C.E.). Object 30-12-25, from a joint British Museum/University Museum Expedition to Ur, Iraq. Courtesy the University of Pennsylvania Museum of Archaeology and Anthropology.

Feel this slab of the threshold, brought from far away!
Advance toward the Temple, the House of Ishtar,
That no other king, no one else, was able to imitate!
Climb up and stroll on Uruk's ramparts,
Inspect the foundations, observe the lines of bricks:
Are they not indeed hand-baked?
And did not the Seven Sages themselves lay the base?
Three hundred hectares of city, and as many of gardens,
And as many of virgin soil belong to the Temple.
Behold! In these thousand hectares you see all of Uruk!

Go now and seek the copper casket,
Turn the bronze ring,
Open the secret compartment,
And pull out the lapis-lazuli tablets in order to read
How Gilgamesh went through his many trials.[26]

The poet apostrophizes the reader, urging him or her to look, consider, feel, advance, climb, stroll, inspect, seek, open, pull out, and read. In a vertiginous, self-perpetuating circle, the reader is told to travel through the city of which he is reading, in order to discover a text (the one he now holds in his hands) that will tell him how to accomplish a series of tasks so as to learn about King Gilgamesh's adventures. As we begin to read, we are already obeying the poet's injunction; we are already part of the poem. From the first words of the first tablet, we, the readers, become Gilgamesh's fellow travelers.

Obviously, a distinction must be made between the poem's first readers and ourselves, reading in the twenty-first century. The *Gilgamesh* epic, written in an Akkadian dialect from the second millennium B.C.E., is probably a recasting of a series of earlier Akkadian poems, based in turn on ancient Sumerian texts. The epic as we know it can therefore be said to have been composed over several centuries, revised and shaped in the end by a scholar-priest whose name has come down to us as Sin-leqi-unninni. Its first readers would have been familiar with the story and would have followed the wanderings of King Gilgamesh and his friend much as if the poem had been a strict historical or documentary chronicle. Over the centuries, however, this familiarity acquired a kaleidoscopic mythical reading. It must be remembered that Mesopotamia was a multilingual society, or several multilingual societies, so that, for instance, at the end of the third and beginning of the second millennium B.C.E., Sumerian judges would record in Akkadian (and not in their own tongue) the testimonies given in court, and legal documents would often carry their translations. This sharing and overlapping of at least two languages and cultures changed and enriched over the centuries parallel interpretations of the ancient stories. For example, the god Enlil, a divinity often present in Mesopotamian narratives (he is associated with Ninurta, the war god, in the *Epic of Gilgamesh*), was for the Sumerians of the second millennium not the protector of any specific city but rather an all-inspiring, ecumenical god. In contrast, for the Akkadians he was a destructive force, responsible for monstrous flooding. Thus the god's hallowed breath was read as life-giving by the former and life-taking by the latter. In the first millennium and with the preeminence of the Amorite kings, new layers of meaning were attached to the old vocabularies, and under the influence of Vedic culture from India and Aramean culture from Syria, figures such as Enlil acquired newer and unexpected features.[27] In the eyes of successive generations, the stories grew and changed, not as much through rewriting as through rereading, through the adding of contextual layers that gradually overlapped, enriched, or eliminated previous ones.

The landscape over which Gilgamesh and his readers traveled—the desert around the city of Uruk, the mountains beyond, the woods and groves—would have changed as the travelers themselves changed, and with them the act of traveling through the story. The awe experienced by the first recipients of the text to whom it was read aloud by scribes, feeling that they had been invited to share the royal adventures, would have gradually become an exercise in collective memory, as well as an aesthetic pleasure, a capacity for evaluating the narrative technique honed by generations of readers and listeners. The audience was still required to accompany the heroes on their perilous journey, but after many readings the magic must have seemed tamer, the adventures tinged with religious allegory, the poem accompanied by philosophical glosses and learned commentaries. In the last days of the great Mesopotamian civilizations, whether at the time of the fall of Ur in around 2000

B.C.E. or that of the fall of Babylon in around 1600 B.C.E., the *Epic of Gilgamesh* remained, no doubt, a thing of wonder, but also a point of reference, a touchstone for those various overlapping cultures: what we today would call a classic.

All those generations of readers, as well as our own, share at least one peculiar feature. King Gilgamesh, the audience is told from the start, has long completed his earthly journey, and the poet (as the last of the eleven tablets proves) has long composed the final words of his chronicle. The reader, however, has yet to set off, but with the advantage (or disadvantage) of knowing both the route and the final destination. The text created the landscape to be traveled, and did away with the real distance between places and the attendant labors of physical travel. By the eighteenth century B.C.E., the fact of reader and writer being brought together by the craft of words was explicitly stated, so that reading and writing consciously became a means of transport across space. "Bulattal brought me your news," says a letter written in the early 1700s B.C.E. in the Zagros Mountains and sent to the settlement of Shemshara, "and I am much delighted: I had the impression that you and I had met and we had embraced."[28] The words on the tablet brought the writer to the destination along the route that the text had charted: in this way, the reader became the text's privileged traveler.

And yet, from the early days of *Gilgamesh* onward, it can be said that if we readers are travelers, we are not, however, pioneers: the path we take has been trodden before, and the maps of the country have already been drawn (even if in the days of the hypertext, in certain cases, the maps can be modified by the reader). Conscious of overcoming the limitations of physical geography and historical time, readers allow for another geography and history as they advance through the text, a space and a time that belong to the textual narrative and are reenacted in the readers' eye.

This was true then and is true now. In spite of rhetorical rules of composition that attempt to limit or govern the construction of the narrated time and space, readers become increasingly aware that the game of "suspension of disbelief" into which they enter with the writer forces them to accept new physical laws for the world of each specific book. Readers must accept that vast territories of the imagination can be crossed in the space of one paragraph, and centuries can go by in a single sentence. They can be delayed in one place over dozens of pages, or they can spend a literate eternity in the course of just one volume. The reading experience mirrors the fluctuating impression of being in this dreamlike world, of distance and proximity, of past, present, and future. Like the Lilliputian king who is aware of the passing of the clock's hand marking the seconds, or like the souls in Dante's Heaven for whom all space is one single point, readers experience in their reading the inklings of unreality of everyday life, the elasticity of time or the changing forms of space. Whether wandering through unreal cities or entering undiscovered countries, whether trying to reach the shores of Ithaca or lighting out for the Territory, whether discovering ice for the first time or being promised an ever-postponed excursion to the lighthouse, our routes are signposted and a guide (reliable or not) is always at hand, reminding us of the moments that lasted for days or years, and of the landscapes too small or too vast for comprehension.

After Gilgamesh's beloved, Enkidu, has died, Gilgamesh decides to travel to the Realm of the Dead to find him, and the reader goes with him. "Which is the way to the Realm of the Dead?" Gilgamesh asks. "I must know! Is it the sea? the mountains? I will go there!"[29] So will the reader, setting off on what is one of the first otherworldly narratives of our history, combining in one story the knowledge and pain of loss, the mad desire to reverse time and to bring back the dead, the unconvincing conviction that beyond the horizon lies a place where we will find what we are missing and where all will be well. Sea and mountains are the landscapes we know, and from high up in the mountains and down and across the sea Gilgamesh (and we, the readers) will travel, through the poem, from the first to the last clay tablet or page. Reading allows us to experience our intuitions as facts, and to transform the moving through experience into a recognizable passage through the text.

The Road of Life

Lest you should ponder the road of life.

—Proverbs 5:6

Some three thousand years after *Gilgamesh*, Dante tells us that, halfway along the road of life, he found himself in a dark forest. Here begins what is perhaps the most famous travel narrative in Western literature, one that will take us, Dante's readers, through

Entrance to the Wood of the Suicides. Canto XIII from
the Divine Comedy in *Opere di Dante Alighieri* (Venice: A. Zatta, 1757).
Courtesy the University of Pennsylvania Rare Book and Manuscript Library.

three otherworldly realms that, by means of Dante's words, have acquired a permanent and tangible geography in our imagination. In societies with roots in Christianity, to speak of Hell, Purgatory, and Paradise is to make use, consciously or not, of Dante's logbook. Beginning with the dark forest where the straight path is lost, a place "almost as bitter as death itself," the reader follows Dante down into the infernal circles and up through the cleansing terraces and across the Heavens to the Empyrean. To think back on that forest, Dante tells us—a forest wild and rough and dense—renews in his mind the fear he felt at the time, a fear that the reader is now compelled to feel as well. And yet, however hard the task, Dante knows that he must tell of the things he saw, "for the sake of the good [he] there discovered."[30] Implicit in this declared intention is a gift to the reader: it is for us that Dante will force himself to return to the scene of his perilous travels, for us that he will follow again the arduous path that led him deep into the earth and high into the heavens, for us that he will struggle to reach once more the instant of supreme vision. "You had best undertake another journey,"[31] says Virgil to Dante at their first encounter, and offers his ward a journey that is not the one Dante intended, straight from the dark forest to the top of the blessed mountain, but one through the realms of the Afterlife, first seeing and suffering with his body, and then in his mind and through his poetry. From the first words of the first canto, we, the readers of that journey, become Dante's fellow travelers.

As in the case of *Gilgamesh*, our role as travelers differs from those of both the pilgrim and the poet. "Nel mezzo del cammin di nostra vita": we understand that these first words are the starting point of the narrative, but this is only true in a literal sense. The journey itself started much earlier. The beginning we are given to read is already *halfway along the road of our life*; it is only at this middle point that we are invited to join the traveler, after a lengthy stretch has already been covered, well before the book's opening, through landscapes and episodes of the poet's early life that Dante has chosen not to chronicle in the *Commedia*. We begin traveling in what medieval rhetoric formalized as *in media res*, in the middle of the thing itself.

In one other important sense we are deprived of an actual beginning. The action referred to in "mi ritrovai per una selva oscura" ("I found myself in a dark forest") has taken place long ago, in Dante's sinful past. The adventures are now over, the terror and the surprise are distant memories, the repentance and the revelation have already happened, and the pilgrim has returned to earth, ready to bear witness. (In medieval terms, "pilgrimage" denoted a journey to the shrine and back, not a one-way passage.) Though the voyage was dangerous, the realms uncharted, the outcome unforeseen, all has now been resolved, the goal has been reached, the return to port safely effected—and all this is implied in those very first words of the poem. As the reader knows, for the poem to exist, the pilgrim must have survived, like the messengers in Job, to tell the story.

As readers of Dante's poem, we are therefore privileged witnesses. From the very start, we are promised a happy outcome, since that is the meaning of the title, *Commedia*: a story that ends happily. We know that by the end of *Paradiso*'s final canto the traveler will have reached his destination and will be ready to return home; indeed, that he has returned home to give an account of himself on paper. However, unlike his readers who even on their first venture are somehow aware of the *Commedia*'s layout, Dante, lost in the dark forest, knows nothing of what awaits him: nothing of the three dreadful beasts that will bar his path, nothing of the ghostly presence that will reveal itself as his appointed guide, nothing of the abominable and blissful souls ahead, nothing of the ultimate and ineffable bliss with which his prodigious adventures will be rewarded.

Knowing all this and having such an advantage, will we, the readers, be equal to the task? Will we be able to become worthy travel companions of so extraordinary an adventurer? To accomplish his journey, as we know, Dante the man has become Dante the pilgrim, who in turn has become Dante the poet, the chronicler of his adventures. And we, as followers of Dante's journey, accepting the role now assigned to us, must in turn lose our ordinary identity and become pilgrims ourselves, transformed through the act of reading into necessary characters in the story, addressed by Dante, over and over again, to warn us, guide us, instruct us, beseech us to reflect and to do our enlightened best. "Every path leading to a spiritual realization," wrote the twentieth-century art historian Titus Burckhardt, "demands from whoever undertakes it the stripping of the habitual 'I' in order to become truly oneself, a transformation that is accompanied by the sacrifice of apparent riches and vain pretensions; that is to say, by the sacrifice of humiliation, of the struggle against the passions of which the old 'I' is made."[32] That is certainly the case of Dante the pilgrim, but it is also true of the reader. In order to follow Dante, we must strip ourselves of our everyday identity, we must leave aside the comforts of common sense and familiar references, we must sacrifice our solid and reassuring notions of factual reality, and we must humbly submit to the rules and resolutions set down by the poet for our guidance. But can we do this?

Dante is very aware of our difficulties in this respect, and as he is about to enter the First Heaven, guided by the terrible smile of Beatrice, he speaks to the readers, his traveling companions, in warning terms:

> Oh you who in your little boat
> Longing to hear, have followed on my keel
> That sings along the way,
>
> Turn to see again your own home shores
> Don't enter the open sea, or well you might
> By losing sight of me, be lost yourselves.[33]

E. R. Curtius, who gave a brief history of the metaphor of the world as book in his famous study of the persistence of classical imagery in European literature,[34] noted that many were the Latin poets who compared the craft of writing to that of sailing—Propertius, Manilius, Horace, and Statius among several others. In the second book of the *Georgics* Virgil speaks of setting sail ("vela dare"), and toward the end of the fourth he speaks of bringing the sails down ("vela trahere").[35] This circular motion, beginning and ending the act of sailing forth, is essential to the idea of traveling through a text. Travel narratives, factual or allegorical, have this in common: they carry implicit in them their conclusion, and their point of departure assumes a point of arrival. Every travel narrative declares that "in my end is my beginning," since, once having arrived, the traveler will begin the voyage again by telling of his or her adventures. In fact, the very purpose of Dante's pilgrimage is to begin again, and this time not with fearful steps but with fiery words. "She who, for our sake, left her footprints in Hell," says Dante of Beatrice: the same might be said of Dante by his readers. The voyage was made for us, for the sake of the story.

Dante's story, then, is both a landscape and a map; or rather a series of landscapes whose map is unfurled as the traveler advances through it, walking or climbing, flying on the back of a monster or being rowed across hellish waters, guided by Virgil or Statius up Mount Purgatory or carried timelessly through the Heavens by Beatrice. So precise, so vivid, so cartographically exact are Dante's descriptions of the realms he crosses that the twenty-four-year-old Galileo, not the least empirical of men, was able to deliver, in 1588, two scientific lectures on the situation and size of Dante's Hell. "If it has been difficult and admirable," wrote Galileo, "for men to have succeeded, after lengthy observations, endless vigils, dangerous navigations, to measure and establish the intervals between the heavens, their fast movements and their slow ones, and their relationships, and the size of heavenly bodies whether near or far away, and the sites of earth and sea (all things that, either entirely or for the most part, are prey to the senses)—then how much more marvelous must we deem the study and description of the site and size of Hell which, buried in the entrails of the Earth, hidden from our senses, is known to no one and lies beyond all experience."[36] For Galileo, as for Dante, the imaginary world, just like the physical world itself, can be mapped and explored by the reader. The book is a world through which we can travel because the world is a book that we can read.

There are, however, for a reader, various modes of traveling. Dante, reader of both Augustine and Virgil, was conscious of the chasm between the affections derived from literary reading and those that should be elicited by the books of God. The *Commedia* can be understood as the process by which the passage from one to the other is learned: from the intellectual and affective apprehension of Virgil (and the other books in Dante's library), to the drama of Dante's own life under the authorship of God. Certainly, for Dante, one of God's books cannot be read properly without aid of the other: the world and the word mirror one another metaphorically, and though intellectual skill is not enough, and can even be a hindrance to authentic revelation, a practiced reader can acquire the capacity of self-awareness that will allow Dante (as Virgil says to him when he leaves him in the hands of Beatrice) to "crown and miter thee over thyself."[37] Before he emerged from the dark forest, the delights of this earth had more attraction for Dante than the promised delights of Heaven, and even as he mourned the transient body of his Beatrice he failed to read in her mortal ruins the image of her superior beauty after her transfiguration. As Dante the pilgrim advances through the three perceptible realms, the poetic or intellectual image of the world as text becomes more and more concrete, blending the characteristics of both earthly and heavenly beauty, until it takes on what Dante calls "a universal shape"[38] and becomes the final metaphor. For Dante, when reaching the promised vision in the Empyrean, after seeing Paradise as a specious succession of Heavens—in the guise of a blessed light, a rose, a wheel within a wheel—the ultimate reality proves to be the image of a book.

Dante's pilgrimage is therefore not only an act of material travel, a displacement in space, but also one in time, as in Augustine's reading of a psalm. Unlike the physical traveler who simply follows the path forward, Dante the pilgrim, like a curious and reflective reader, while moving along the road from the first to the last page, allows himself to go back, to retrace explored territory, to recall, foretell, and associate events past, present, and future, leafing back and forth through God's writings, where "that which in the universe seems separate and scattered" is "gathered and bound by love in one single volume."[39] It should be noted, however, that Dante cannot read this crowning book, since in the presence of the final vision his verbal skill "seems even less than that of a suckling infant."[40] (Two centuries after Dante, Sandro Botticelli was commissioned to illustrate the entire *Commedia*. He never finished the work. As if echoing Dante's avowed impossibility to put perfectly into words the divine revelation, Botticelli seems to have recognized the equal impossibility of putting perfectly into images Dante's concluding words: the last sheet of all, now unfortunately lost, was left blank.)[41]

For Dante's contemporaries, the image of the reader as traveler carried, by and large, an active and positive connotation. Reading was a beneficial labor, if directed toward the right goal and performed in the right spirit, allowing the intellect to understand what the spirit intuits through love. In this sense, all human beings were meant to be travelers, which is perhaps why, in the biblical tradition, God preferred the offerings of the nomadic herdsman Abel to those of the sedentary crop grower Cain, and punished Cain, after his crime, by forcing him to become a wanderer himself.[42] But there were many shades to this interpretation. Readers who committed themselves to the exploration of a text had the qualities of an adventurer, an explorer, an intrepid seafarer who could either, like Jason, pursue a worthy cause and bring back home the Golden Fleece[43] or, like the *Commedia*'s Ulysses, pursue a merely reckless goal in a "mad flight"[44] from which there is no return, condemning himself to burn in Dante's Hell throughout eternity for his audacity. Travel could also be a punishment, as in the case of the Wandering Jew who, in the medieval legend, is condemned

to wander the earth until the Second Coming for having denied Christ rest when he was carrying the Cross past the Jew's
doorstep.[45] The reader-travelers could be rewarded for their
efforts or punished for their gall.

But, in its most praiseworthy sense, traveling, like reading,
was a pilgrimage that mirrored the pilgrimage of human life. It
was a journey of purgation, beset by temptation and suffering,
but the reward for the upright traveler was the "better place"
promised in the Hereafter. As early as the sixth century, the
Ecclesiastical Council of Mâcon prescribed for a bishop who
had committed murder a fifteen-year penitence of scripture
study and, after that, "a pilgrimage for the remainder of his
life."[46] Reading to cleanse the soul and traveling to cleanse the
body were seen as two complementary actions that the sinner needed to perform in order to be saved. Taking as his text
Christ's words in the Gospel of John (14:6), "I am the way, the
truth and the life," Saint Augustine composed a sermon in
which he entreated sinners to take the right path. "If they did
so, there was assurance for them, since they could run without
getting lost! How they are to be pitied when, on the contrary,
they hurry on without keeping to the path! It is better to limp
along the path than to walk with a steady foot when missing
the path altogether."[47] Already in an earlier sermon, Augustine
had noted: "Our spirit has two feet—one of the intellect and
one of the affect, or of cognition and love—and we must move
both so that we may walk in the right way."[48] In the first canto
of the *Inferno*, Dante tells the reader that, after emerging from

the dark forest, he walked along a desert strand, "the right foot always the lower."[49] Countless commentaries have attempted to explain this limping foot, but it may simply be that Dante, a thorough reader of Augustine, remembered the sermon and translated it into the circumstances of his pilgrimage, in order better to allegorize his journey and also to suggest to the reader that a slow perusal of the poem "in the right way" is better than reading quickly but "missing the path altogether." This is the explicit warning that Thomas Aquinas gives Dante in the Heaven of the Prudent: to think carefully and go through his words step by step. "And let this ever be as lead to your feet, / To make you move slowly, like a tired man."[50] A pilgrim, like a reader, must advance gradually.

"Dante is a pilgrim, Ulysses an explorer," noted a celebrated Dante critic.[51] Dante, glossing one of his own sonnets, explained that "*pilgrim* can be understood in one of two ways, one broad, the other restricted: in a broad sense, pilgrim is anyone who is far from his homeland; in a restricted sense, pilgrim only means he who travels toward the House of Saint James [the sanctuary of Saint James of Compostela]."[52] Dante, who wrote his *Commedia* in exile, must have known in what broad sense he was himself a pilgrim. He must have felt the proximity between his itinerant life and his itinerant reading, and known the bitterness (as he says in the *Commedia*) of eating "alien bread tasting like salt" and of climbing "up and down alien stairs." "I have wandered like a beggar through virtually all the regions to which this tongue of ours extends," he says in the *Convivio*,[53] reading his way through Italy. During the twenty long years of exile, until the last day of his life, Dante's library consisted of the few books he dragged with him from one refuge to another, to which were occasionally added the ones his hosts would lend him—a changing collection that reflected the different stages and experiences of the various sites of his banishment.

Augustine had noted that reading was a form of travel, "not of places but of affections."[54] For Dante it was both. Reading was for him the literal exploration of the geography of his elected authors—Saint Augustine's Rome and Carthage and the Celestial Jerusalem, Statius's Ethiopia, Virgil's Italy, the otherworldly realms of Saint Thomas Aquinas and Saint Bonaventure—together with their overlaid cartography of affection and experience. There was perhaps a point, toward the end of his life, when Dante no longer knew whether his *Commedia* was an intricate map of his life or whether his life was a hesitant sketch for his *Commedia*. Many a reader feels the same.

The journey that reading offered Dante (and Augustine and Bonaventure) was one of preparation, of comparison, of awareness, a journey measured by what Augustine called "the particles of sand in the glass of time," at the end of which God might at last open the pages of his book. It is Christ, Augustine acknowledges, addressing God himself, who "is your Word. . . . In him the whole treasury of wisdom and knowledge is stored up, and these are the treasures I seek in your books."[55] Perhaps, for the right reader, almost any book holds this promise.

Perhaps the journey that true reading offers can lead to this treasury, to the "ultimate good" that Aristotle and his Christian interpreters, such as Dante, saw as the end of all human purpose, even before the soul's journey to rejoin the godhead after the last breath is drawn.

Not so, argued Saint Bonaventure, skeptical about the success of any reading journey that did not entail the agonies of true faith. A generation before Dante's, in a short treatise entitled *The Journey of the Mind to God*, Bonaventure concluded that it is not through "studious reading" that the mind reaches divine revelation (that is to say, "how such things come about") but through "prayerful groaning." Not the journey of life, but the journey's end will grant us understanding. "Let us die, then," he says, "and pass over into darkness."[56] Saint Augustine, too, reaches this realization that reading is useless for fully apprehending either the Book of the World or the Book of the Word. These volumes are ultimately inscrutable. And Dante, at the end of his *Commedia*, echoes Saint Augustine's words: "How short-reaching my words, and how faintly / Do they reflect my purpose! Compared to what I saw / It barely is enough to call it scarce."[57] For Bonaventure, for Augustine, for Dante, reading serves the purpose of helping the pilgrim along the road of revelation, pricking his curiosity and his conscience, up to the page before last. There its usefulness must stop, because, as occurs in any text we call great, the ultimate understanding must escape us. We have arrived, but at a place so unknown that no words exist to describe it.

Traveling the Web

Others apart sat on a hill retir'd,
In thoughts more elevate, and reason'd high
Of providence, foreknowledge, will, and fate,
Fix'd fate, free will, foreknowledge absolute,
And found no end, in wand'ring mazes lost.
—John Milton, *Paradise Lost*, II:557–61

The power of a metaphor can be assessed both by the degree
to which it conjures up the idea at its source and by the de-

Codex or computer? Photographs by John Hubbard.

gree to which it enriches or contaminates further ideas. The metaphor of the world as book appropriately confirms our impression that the space around us carries meaning and that every landscape tells a story, illuminating the act of reading with the sense of deciphering not only the words on the page but the world itself. World and text, travel and reading, are concomitant images, easily evoked in the imagination. Both travel and reading unfold in time, both world and text define a space. Life as a journey is, as we have seen, one of our most ancient metaphors; because to read is to journey through a book, the image links all three activities, so that each one— reading, living, traveling—borrows from and enriches the others. The reader is therefore both the traveler through the world and the traveler through life, except, as Orhan Pamuk concluded in his novel *Silent House*: "You can't start out again in life, that's a carriage ride you only take once, but with a book in your hand, no matter how confusing and perplexing it might be, once you've finished it, you can always go back to the beginning; if you like, you can read it through again, in order to figure out what you couldn't understand before, in order to understand life."[58]

In the introduction to his collected travel essays, *Nomad's Hotel*, Cees Nooteboom quotes the twelfth-century Arab traveler Ibn al-Arabi: "The origin of existence is movement. Immobility can have no part in it, for if existence was immobile it would return to its source, which is the Void. That is why the voyaging never stops, in this world or in the hereafter."[59] As

Nooteboom understands it, Ibn al-Arabi equates living with traveling, aware of the meaning of coming to a halt.

Nooteboom is a fair example of the twenty-first-century traveler. On the one hand, a resigned adventurer for whom the practical experience of crossing space and time is charged with the bewilderment of speed and the dreariness of delays and waiting, a sort of unholy mingling of promptness and procrastination. On the other, a traditional seeker for what is in essence an intellectual and affective experience, a preconceived literary notion of what travel in the abstract is, a sense of transition tinged with a willingness to be surprised, comforted, and challenged. "It is impossible to prove and yet I believe it," Nooteboom writes at the beginning of his travel book about the roads to Santiago, "there are some places in the world where one is mysteriously magnified on arrival or departure by the emotions of all those who have arrived and departed before. Anyone possessed of a soul so light feels a gentle tug in the air around the Schreierstoren, the Sorrower's Tower in Amsterdam, which has to do with the accumulated sadness of those left behind. It is a sadness," Nooteboom adds, "we do not experience today: our journeys no longer take years to complete, we know exactly where it is we are going, and our chances of coming back are so much greater."[60]

It is perhaps because of this, that the image of the reader-traveler is no longer as resonant today as it was in the past. What has changed, as Nooteboom makes clear, is not the idea of reading as travel but the meaning of travel itself. For Dante's contemporaries, travel mirrored precisely the essential act of living, of unknown duration, perilous and many times bitter, fraught with deadly temptations. "I am a stranger on earth, a passerby, like all my ancestors, an exile, an uneasy traveler in this brief life," wrote Petrarch in one of his letters,[61] barely half a century after Dante's journey. We, however, no longer carry a constant sense of transience within us, at least not in the essential way in which Petrarch and Dante felt it. Everything in our societies today incites us to believe that we are quasi-immortal beings, preserved in an eternal present, and that all our activities (reading included) must be conclusive in an absolute sense. We believe only in certainties. Change for us is not a passage that builds up the province of our memory while reducing that of our expectation, as Augustine understood it, but a leap from one moment to another on which the previous moments cast no shadow, while the ones to come are never brought to mind. This persistent instantaneity convinces us that we exist only here and now, in whatever circle we happen to find ourselves, with no sense of debt to the past or of the overlapping of experience, except as conceited outposts of progress. It creates for us the illusion of a constant present, seized in the emblem of the flickering screen always open before us, suggesting that, since we have entrusted our memory to a machine, we can disregard the past in all its manifestations (libraries, archives, the recollection of our elders, our own ability to recall) and so dismiss the consequences of our actions. If today reading is a form of travel, it is only in the sense of passing timelessly from place to place, ignoring differences of latitude and longitude, pretending that everything occurs for us and under our gaze, and that we can always be informed of all that happens, wherever we might find ourselves. Nooteboom remarks that "anyone who is constantly travelling is always somewhere else, and therefore always absent," and he disapprovingly quotes Pascal's dictum that "the root of the world's misfortune lies in the fact that human beings are unable to remain in one room for twenty-four hours."[62] Today's travel partakes of both sides: a constant absence (for most of our nomadic race) through physical displacement, and a constant claustrophobic presence in workplaces and shopping malls, planes and trains, airport lobbies and tourist sites.

Nooteboom attempts to escape this paradox by declaring that his travel is in fact another, richer way of being at home, "namely with myself."[63] Four centuries earlier, Michel de Montaigne agreed with him. His physical travels, he wrote, could be interrupted at any point; "they are not founded on great hopes, each day is in fact its own goal. And the voyage of my life is conducted in the same way." Therefore, he added: "I most often travel alone, and take pleasure in entertaining myself. It happens as in my dreams: by dreaming them, I entrust them to my memory." The experience of travel, for Montaigne as for Nooteboom, is like the experience of reading, an exercise in self-reflection.

But for most travelers today, an essential part of the experience is to avoid being with themselves. E. M. Forster's too-famous advice "only connect"[64] has taken the shape of a mindless interconnectedness, the feeling that by means of the World Wide Web we are never alone, never required to account for ourselves, never obliged to reveal our true identity. We travel in herds, we chat in groups, we acquire friends on Facebook, we dread an empty room and the sight of a single shadow on our wall. We feel uncomfortable reading alone; we want our reading too to be "interconnected," sharing comments onscreen, being directed by best-seller lists that tell us what others are reading, and by reader's guides added by the publisher to the original text, suggesting questions to ask and answers to give. Nooteboom says that when he was young and inexperienced, he "chose movement"; only later on, "when I understood more, I realised I would be able, within this movement, to find the silence necessary in order to write."[65] Most of us, however, dread silence because in silence we might be forced to observe, to reflect on past experience, to think.

The act of reading a single line, deeply and comprehensively, carried for Saint Augustine the echo of all our libraries, past, present, and future, each word harking back to Babel and forward to the last trumpet. It meant a constant displacement from one acquired experience to the next, a nomadic reading through memory toward desire, conscious of the road traveled and of the road still ahead. Our worldwide reading, precisely because it assumes itself to be worldwide, seems to require no such displacement: everything, we are told, is here always, at the touch of a finger. We don't need to travel toward it because it appears all of a sudden, we don't need to commit it to memory because our electronic memories perform that duty in our name, we don't need to explore and sift through endless volumes because search engines will find our quarries for us. Nor do we need to claim a traveler's freedom and responsibility in the act of reading: the rules and regulations of our technological apparatuses set strict parameters for us to follow and assume the praise or blame. Reading an electronic book, Dante's *Commedia* in its digital edition for instance,[66] while possessing a uniform worldwide quality and proclaiming the possibilities of unlimited navigation, is in fact far more restricted and controlled than Dante's own codex reading. This is partly because Dante and his contemporaries were conscious that, as readers, they were with the author on a journey that they would enrich with their own experience, with no other limitations than those established by the text itself and by their own capabilities. We instead, readers of an electronic text, set off through scrolling panels that lay before us enclosures of writing all identical to each other. We skim down an always present page surrounded not by space left for commentary but, in many cases, by preordained links to other pages, as well as distracting advertising. On the screen, we lack the material sense of physically following the story, unlike that the experience of holding a codex in our hands. Useful it is, of course, but it is limiting as well. As travelers in cyberspace we need to be more aware of these limitations and to find ways of reclaiming our traveler's freedom.

In a recent online publication analyzing the evolution of Google and its effects on the common reader, the French electronics analyst Jean Sarzana, together with his colleague Alain Pierrot, compared traditional book reading and electronic reading to different forms of travel. "With the book," the authors wrote, "we sail like the Greeks did, with the coast always in sight. The electronic text allows us to pass on to satellite travel, and to see the Earth from far, far away."[67] I would say that the contrary is true. Reading a codex held in our hands, conscious of its physical characteristics and material presence, we associate freely the page we are reading with other parts of the book, and also with other books; we reconstruct arguments and characters in our mind; we connect ideas and theories in a vast horizonless mental space. Reading electronically, we are, for the most part, "in wand'ring mazes lost."

The solid book of paper and ink is the ground we journey through, a starting point for commentary and conjecture. Its double, the book developed in our mind, is, as Augustine noted, a journal map of the original, a mental text made of past, present, and future reading, of recollection and anticipation. The electronic book, however, is not grounded; it is, by definition, virtual, and this apparent lack of solidity, this ghostly presence, accomplishes only up to a point our traditional mnemonic function, and though it performs the mental traveling we seek, it does it for its own sake, as it were, scrolling on without us needing to become conscious of the progress or take responsibility for it. These are not comparisons of value; they are comparisons of nature, of methods not better or worse but merely different from one another. Dante's reading was like Ulysses's sailing, far into the main, "to experience the unpeopled world behind the Sun."[68] Except that, unlike Ulysses, Dante knew that there was always a first page to which he could unceasingly return. If we are to follow the expectations of our mercantile society, to perform first and foremost a technological task of which one of the byproducts is reading, today we must hug the electronic shore.

It may be that, in our increasingly gadget-driven society, we have lost a certain sense of why we read, as we may have lost a certain sense of why we travel. Robert Louis Stevenson famously declared, "For my part, I travel not to go anywhere, but to go. I travel for travel's sake. The great affair is to move."[69] He was speaking to an audience for whom travel had a destination, and also a home to which the traveler might safely return to profit from the experience. Today's travel has no destination. Its purpose is not to move but to stand still, to remain in the here and now or, what amounts to the same thing, to move almost instantaneously from site to site, so that there is no passage from one point to another, either in space or in time, much as in our new reading habits. Unfortunately, such methods affect not only travel and reading. They affect our thoughts as well, our reflective capacities, our intellectual muscles. Our thinking functions require not only awareness of ourselves but also awareness of our passage through the world, and awareness of our passage through the pages of a book. This was an ability which we developed after the age of Gilgamesh's tablets, and which we have relinquished in the age of the screen. Now we must once more learn to read slowly, profoundly, comprehensively, whether on paper or on the screen: to travel in order to return with what we've read. Only then will we, in the deepest sense, be able to call ourselves readers.

CHAPTER 2

THE READER IN THE IVORY TOWER

Reading as Alienation from the World

What tranquil life

Leads he who escapes the worldly din

And seeks the hidden path wherein

Are found the few who in this world were wise.

—Fray Luis de León,

Song of the Solitary Life

The Melancholy Tower

It is an uneasy lot at best, to be what we call highly taught and yet not to enjoy: to be present at this great spectacle of life and never to be liberated from a small hungry shivering self—never to be fully possessed by the glory we behold, never to have our consciousness rapturously transformed into the vividness of a thought, the ardor of a passion, the energy of an action, but always to be scholarly and uninspired, ambitious and timid, scrupulous and dim-sighted.

—George Eliot, *Middlemarch*

In front of a cosy fire, a curled-up dog at his feet, a man in a green dressing gown sits in his reading chair, but he isn't reading. His book lies closed on an adjacent wooden chest. His head, wrapped in a pink scarf for warmth and comfort, leans against a white pillow. His right hand holds his robe, his left hand is tucked inside, as if to keep warm or to feel the beatings of his heart. His eyes are shut, so that he does not see (or does not choose to see) the nun approaching him with a prayer book and a rosary. The nun is perhaps an allegory of faith, summoning the man to his spiritual duties. A large side window shows a couple strolling through a bucolic landscape in the world of worldly pleasures. The shape of the picture is a sort of curved trapezoid and it lends the setting the appearance of a room in a tower. Stenciled on the patterned floor in Gothic letters is a single word: Accidia.

The image is part of a table top painted by Hieronymus Bosch in the first decades of the sixteenth century, and now in the Prado Museum in Madrid. The entire composition depicts, in a circle, the seven deadly sins, with a vigilant Christ in the center, rising over the warning: "Cave, cave, deus videt" ("Beware, beware, God sees"). Four medallions, one in each corner of the table top, illustrate, clockwise, the death of a sinner, the Last Judgment, the reception in Paradise, and the punishments in Hell. Our sleeper illustrates sloth, the sin known in the Middle Ages as that of the midday demon.

A second Bosch painting, known as *The Peddler* or *The Prodigal Son*, does not seem, at first instance, to deal with the

Hieronymus Bosch, "Accidia." Detail from *The Table of the Seven Deadly Sins* (c. 1485). Courtesy the Museo Nacional del Prado.

same subject. The traditional titles of this work are misleading: the protagonist is less a peddler than a pilgrim, less one of the shady tramps of Flemish folklore than a man on a spiritual quest. The story of the Prodigal Son coming back to his father is perhaps a more fitting interpretation, since the allegorical reading speaks of the sinner repenting and returning to his Father in Heaven. Two versions exist of this work: one in the Boymans Museum in Rotterdam, another on one of the covering panels of the *Hay-Wagon* triptych in the Prado (a copy also hangs in El Escorial). In both versions, a middle-aged man advances through an everyday landscape of delights and threats. In the Boymans version, he is coming through a village; in the Prado version, he is out in the countryside, about to cross a stream. He is lean and shabbily dressed. One of his legs (an echo perhaps of the difference between "intellectual foot" and "affect foot," mentioned in Chapter 1) is bandaged and slippered. He carries a basket on his back and a stick in his hands. He looks back toward a menacing dog wearing a spiked collar. In the background of the Boymans version is a tower, looming on the horizon above the pilgrim's right shoulder. In the Prado painting, the tower is replaced by a gallows rising ominously on the hill above the pilgrim's head. Gallows and tower share the same ignominious position.

In the Middle Dutch translation of the bestselling *Speculum Humanae Salvationis*, it is stated that a pilgrim must leave his house and take to the road, and that he often has to seek back paths and defend himself against dangerous dogs with a stick.[1]

Less an allegorical pilgrim than Everyman on the road to salvation, Bosch's traveler responds to the late medieval *Devotio Moderna* movement in the Netherlands that called upon men to seek by themselves the road to salvation, trusting in God and guided not by what is set down in books but by their own reading of the world. In this, the pilgrim must be diligent: he must not allow himself to doze or tarry, or take in the words of false preachers, since "the Devil can quote Scripture for his own evil ends." Instead, he must try to make out God's true word in the text of the world, bearing in mind that, to prevent him from rightly following his path, the Devil has set tempta-

Hieronymus Bosch, *The Prodigal Son* (1487–1516). Courtesy the Museo Nacional del Prado.

tions and menaces between the lines of the world's page. One of the common dangers invented by the Devil was a fearful dog. According to Flemish folklore, this devil-dog haunted the roads; it could, however, be driven off with a walking stick, which rendered the creature powerless to pursue its victim across a stream, like the one in the Prado version.

In the background of the Prado version, six of the seven deadly sins are represented: only the sin of sloth (*accidia*, more usually *acedia*) is not enacted. This role is left to the devil-dog. Only once the sinful effect is achieved (as in the acedia painting referred to first) can the devil-dog curl up and sleep. The *Hortulus reginae* of 1487 speaks of acedia as "similar to the bite of a rabid dog"; following its teachings, preachers warned their flocks that acedia is like the bite of a contagious dog, "a seminal vice that made one susceptible to all the others."[2] An echo of this meaning can be heard in Winston Churchill's reference to his acedia, depression, or melancholia as "a black dog." Modern psychoanalytic parlance has retained the expression.

It is not easy to distinguish between states of "black dog," acedia, depression, and melancholia; depending on the context, all can appear in a positive or a negative light.[3] The ancient Greeks ascribed melancholia to the god Saturn and to one of the five bodily humors, black bile. According to legend, in the fifth century B.C.E. the philosopher Democritus, in order to escape from the follies and distractions of the world, set himself up in a hovel on the outskirts of Abdera in what appeared to be a state of melancholy. The citizens of Abdera, appalled by his conduct, asked Hippocrates to use his medical skills to cure the stranger, whom they took to be a madman. The wise Hippocrates, however, after examining Democritus, turned to the people and told them that it was they, not the philosopher, who were mad, and that they should all imitate his conduct and retire from the world to reflect in worthy solitude.[4] Hippocrates took sides with the man who, bitten by acedia, retired to meditate on the world of which he wanted no part.

Early Christians understood that God is best encountered in isolation. Human intellect was a faculty given to us in order to assist us in our faith: not to clarify the unclarifiable mysteries but to construct a logical scaffolding to support them. The evidence of things unseen would not, by reflection and reasoning, render those things visible, but they would allow the thinker, the scholar, the reader (in the case of those who could read) to ruminate and build upon such evidence, granting the sinner-pilgrim clear sight to peruse the book of the world. For that reason, the isolation of religious men and women, in cells and caves and inhospitable deserts, assisted the work willed by God. Sometimes the isolation was accomplished high on a tower erected in inhospitable places, such as the one on which, in the fifth century, Simeon the Stylite, "despairing of escaping the world horizontally, tried to escape it vertically"[5] and spent high above his brethren the last thirty-six years of his life.

But concomitant with this need for seclusion to nourish the inner life ran an undercurrent of guilt, a self-censuring of the very act of quiet thinking. Humankind, the church fathers taught, was meant to use its intellect to understand what could be understood, but there were questions that were not meant to be asked and limits of reasoning that were not meant to be transgressed. Dante charged Ulysses with a guilty curiosity and an arrogant desire to see the unknown world. Retreating into solitude with one's own thoughts might allow for this same sinful desire to arise and, without the counsel and guidance of one's spiritual leaders, remain dangerously unquenched. Therefore, the person seeking God in isolation was to concentrate solely on questions of Christian dogma and remain within the confines of dogmatic theology; pagan authors were dangerous because they distracted, like Ulysses's sirens, from the true course.

In the fourth century, Saint Jerome recounted a dream in a letter to a friend. In order to follow his religious vocation and in compliance with the precepts of the church, Jerome had cut himself off from his family and renounced all earthly pleasures. What he could not bring himself to abandon was his library, which he had collected, "with great care and toil." Wracked by guilt, he would mortify himself and fast, but "only that afterwards I might read Cicero." A short time later, Jerome fell deathly ill. Fever caused him to dream, and he dreamed that his soul was suddenly caught and hauled before God's judgment seat. A voice asked him who he was, and he replied: "I am a Christian." "You lie," said the voice, "you are a Ciceronian." Overcome with dread, Jerome promised God that "if ever again I possess worldly books, or if ever again I read such, I have denied thee."[6] Jerome did not quite comply with his mighty oath, but the story is indicative of the dangers the church perceived in the reader's tower.

Free to meditate on the miseries of the world, the solitary monk (the hermit, the anchorite, like the man in Bosch's *Accidia* fragment) could be seduced into a state of suspended thought, melancholia, or, what was worse, the sin of acedia or sloth, the reverse of Ulysses's sinful thirst for exploring, the shadow side of the philosopher's reflective passion. In the ivory tower, the retired soul could lose himself or herself in inaction. Though melancholia, as has been extensively argued,[7] is, in spite of its symptoms, a creative state, it is difficult to maintain a condition of concentrated meditation without falling into the acedic void. At such moments, the tower loses its nourishing power and becomes a place that drains spiritual and intellectual energy. At the beginning of Goethe's *Faust*, the doctor laments that after reading philosophy and law and medicine, Faust feels himself incapable of accepting the tenets of the faith, and that he is none the wiser. The walls of his tower cramp his soul, and he believes that all his papers and instruments are nothing but "ancestral junk," an image of the world invented by his thoughts. "I take no pleasure in anything now," he says, "For I know I know nothing."[8] He could be voicing the lament for all his intellectual brethren.

The thinkers of the Renaissance tried to turn what the early Christians had seen as the sin of acedia into something like a virtue. The great humanist Marsilio Ficino, commenting on his own melancholia and his habit of withdrawing into solitude ("which only much playing of the lute can sweeten and soften a little"),[9] attempted to withdraw himself from the influence of Saturn and ascribe his state to what Aristotle had called "a singular and divine gift," and Plato before him "a divine furor."[10] Though warning scholars to avoid both phlegm (which blocks the intelligence) and black bile (which causes too much care) "as if they were sailing past Scylla and Charybdis," Ficino concludes that thin black bile is beneficial for the man of letters. To encourage its flow, Ficino gives detailed instructions: not the energetic demeanor of the pilgrim, alert on the road, but the idling disposition of the philosopher, meditative and slow. "When you have got out of bed," advises Ficino, "do not rush right in on your reading or meditation, but for at least half an hour go off and get cleaned up. Then diligently enter your meditation, which you should prolong for about an hour, depending on your strength. Then, put off a little whatever you are thinking about, and in the meantime comb your hair diligently and moderately with an ivory comb, drawing it forty times from the front to the neck. Then rub the neck with a rough cloth, returning only then back to meditating, for two hours or so, or at least for an hour of study."[11] And Ficino concludes: "If you choose to live each day of your life in this way, the author of life himself will help you to stay longer with the human race and with him whose inspiration makes the whole world live."[12] In certain cases and under certain conditions, as a source for philosophical enterprise, melancholy came to be seen as a privileged state, part of the intellectual condition, as well as the source of inspired creation, and the reader, locked away in his or her tower, as a maker in his or her own right.

The search for studious solitude led countless writers and artists, throughout the centuries, to imitate Democritus's isolation. A seemingly endless span of brick-and-mortar towers crosses the literary landscape, from that of Rabelais in Ligugé to those of Hölderlin in Tübingen, Leopardi in Recanati, Jung at Bollingen. Perhaps more than any other, the tower in which Montaigne chose to set up his study has become emblematic of such refuges. Attached to the family chateau in the Bordeaux region, the four-story tower was transformed by Montaigne's father from a defense building into a living space. The ground floor became a chapel, above which Montaigne set up a bedroom to which he could retire after reading in the library, which occupied the floor above, while a large bell rang the hours in the tower's attic. The library was Montaigne's favorite room, where his books, more than a thousand of them, sat on five curved shelves that hugged the circular wall. He tells us that from his windows he has "a view of my garden, my chicken-run, my backyard and most parts of my house. There I can turn over the leaves of this book or that, a bit at a time without order or design. Sometimes my mind wanders off, at others I walk to and fro, noting down and dictating these whims of mine." Privacy was of the essence. "There," Montaigne says, "I have my seat. I assay making my dominion over it absolutely pure, withdrawing this one corner from all intercourse, filial, conjugal and civic. Elsewhere I have but a verbal authority, one essentially impure. Wretched the man (to my taste) who has nowhere in his house where he can be by himself, pay court to himself in private and hide away!"[13]

Even today, the image of the ivory tower retains at times this connotation of allowing the intellectual to retire from the world only better to assume it. In 1966, the Austrian playwright and novelist Peter Handke gave a talk at Princeton entitled "I Am an Inhabitant of the Ivory Tower," in which he opposed his own writing to the German literature that preceded him. "A certain normative conception of literature uses a lovely expression to designate those who refuse to go on telling stories, while seeking new methods to describe the world," Handke said. "It says that they 'live in an ivory tower' and brands them as 'formalists' and 'aesthetes.'" Handke started off his lecture by confessing: "For a long time, literature was for me the means, if not of seeing my inner self clearly, then at least of seeing with more clarity. It helped me to realize that I was there, that I was in the world. Certainly, I had become conscious of myself before dealing with literature, but it was only literature that showed me how this consciousness was not a unique case, not even a case, nor a sickness. Before literature, this self-consciousness had, so to speak, possessed me, it had been something terrible, shameful, obscene; this natural phenomenon seemed to me an intellectual deviance, an infamy, a motive for shame, because I seemed to be alone in this experience. It was only literature that caused my consciousness of this consciousness to be born;

it showed me clearly that I was not a unique example, that others lived the same thing."[14] The intellectual act, performed in the ivory tower, is for Handke (as it has been for Ficino) a means of apprehending our own experience, and of putting the world into words.

Certain metaphors are slow in the making. Even though the image they depict has long been part of a society's *imaginaire*, as an allegorical or symbolic figure, its metaphorical transformation, the actual wording of the image, can come much later. Death visualized as a territory into which we enter for the first time, without knowledge of its geography or of the path to take, appears in the earliest Sumerian texts and runs through almost every literature, until Shakespeare names it the "undiscovered country" from which no traveler returns. Sleep imagined as a stage of dramatic creation in which stories are acted out for the observance of the dreamer is frequently mentioned in the *Epic of Gilgamesh*, in early Egyptian literature, in the Anglo-Saxon poems and on into our time, but only in the sixteenth century does sleep become, in the words of Francisco de Quevedo, a "dramatic author" ("autor de representaciones") who sets up his theater upon the wind. The reader seen as an eccentric withdrawn from the common affairs of society, aloof and supercilious, caring nothing for his fellow citizens, only for the world of books, is mocked in Greek and Roman satires, and turns up (alas) in every era, but it was not until the nineteenth century that the literal term "ivory tower" was used to denote the reader's intellectual sanctum as a place of escape and alienation from the world.[15] In 1837, the French critic Charles-Augustin Sainte-Beuve employed the term, perhaps for the first time, with no negative connotations, to contrast the abstract poetry of Alfred de Vigny with the more politically engaged lyrics of Victor Hugo, imagining the ivory tower as a bookish sanctuary, a place in which the intellectual could work quietly and effectively.

> And Vigny, more secretly,
> As if to his ivory tower, returned before noon.[16]

In the Judeo-Christian tradition, the tower stands as a symbol of either protecting strength or perfect beauty. The Book of Proverbs says, "The name of the Lord is a strong tower: the righteous runneth into it, and is safe,"[17] while Psalm 61 asserts, "For Thou hast been a shelter for me, and a strong tower from the enemy."[18] This image is mirrored in its reverse in the Book of Isaiah as the tower of the proud against which the Lord will victoriously rise.[19] In the Song of Songs, the tower becomes a symbol of the beauty of the beloved (her neck is "a tower of beauty," her breasts are "like towers").[20] Sainte-Beuve's image associated the notions of protection from the outside world and intellectual beauty that ideally make up the reader's resilient, sensuous realm.

But soon afterward, the image of the tower as providing seclusion for studious intellectuals began to be used to depict not their haven but their hiding place, the cell to which they escaped from the duties of the world. In the public imagination, the ivory tower became a refuge set up in opposition to the life in the streets below, and the intellectual there ensconced was seen as a snob, an effete, a shirker, a misanthrope, an enemy of the people.

At the same time that the ivory tower acquired this denigrating connotation, another equally denigrating connotation arose: that of "the masses"—one entity redefining and sustaining the other in a mutual battle of execration. Already in the first century, Seneca, taking sides with the ivory tower intellectual, railed against the ignorant populace or masses. "The best should be preferred most," he wrote, "and yet the masses choose the worst. . . . Nothing is as noxious as listening to the masses, considering as right that which is approved by most, and modelling one's behaviour on those who live, not according to reason, but merely to conform."[21] Implied in the condemnation is the notion that the individual life of the mind should be preferred to the communal rule.

In his important book on intellectuals and the masses, John Carey observes that the varying concepts of "masses" in Hitler's *Mein Kampf* ("as exterminable subhumans, as an inhibited bourgeois herd, as noble workers, as a peasant pastoral") would be familiar to contemporary readers. "The tragedy of *Mein Kampf*," Carey writes, "is that it was not, in many respects, a deviant work but one firmly rooted in European intellectual orthodoxy."[22] The perceived opposition between the thinking, creative elite and the pusillanimous, uncomprehending masses has a long tradition in Europe. Carey begins his history with Ortega y Gasset's *Revolt of the Masses* of 1930, where the Spanish historian notes that while up to 1800 the population of Europe did not exceed 180 million, from then to 1914 it grew to 460 million human beings. Faced with this "flood," "swarm," "inundation," "explosion" (these are a few of the terms used by writers at the time), the individual intellectual felt threatened and saw the very existence of these "masses" as an abomination. At the same time that movements of democratization were advancing in many different social areas, intellectuals were seen to be retreating further and further into their ivory towers, far from what the novelist George Moore called "the blind, inchoate, insatiate Mass."[23] To the tower of the melancholy intellectual, modern imagery opposed the open spaces of the crowds. Toward the former, there developed a certain feeling of resentful claustrophobia, while a feeling akin to a haughty agoraphobia arose toward the faceless masses.

The Studious Prince

Believe you see two points in Hamlet's soul
Unsiezed by the Germans yet.
    —Robert Browning, *Bishop Blougram's Apology*

The double image of the ivory tower, as a haven of studious seclusion (with its attendant dangers) and as a hiding place from responsibility and action (with its ensuing guilt), is perhaps best exemplified by the contradictions perceived over generations of readers in the procrastinating, impulsive, meditative, violent, philosophical, and rash Prince Hamlet.

As the bodies pile up and the tragedy approaches its close, before renouncing forever the power of speech, the mortally wounded Hamlet addresses his friend Horatio and begs of him:

Left: Gustav Gründgens as Hamlet (1936). Courtesy the German Federal Archives.
Right: John Gielgud as Hamlet (1934). Courtesy the Getty Collection.

If thou didst ever hold me in thy heart

Absent thee from felicity awhile,

And in this harsh world draw thy breath in pain,

To tell my story.[24]

Hamlet's dying wish is twofold: that Horatio recount all that has taken place, and that he do this in studious isolation, giving up both his previous carefree existence and his present state of classic despair, drawing his inspiration (or "breath") from the "harsh world" itself. Both actions demand that Horatio return to the past: to go over the events the audience has just witnessed (thus obliging Horatio to become, as it were, the declared author of the play); and, in order to do so, to dwell in the sorrowful moment in which the tragedy concludes. In effect, Hamlet asks Horatio to postpone the moment of his own death (Horatio has only just declared that he is "more an antique Roman than a Dane," that is, that he will commit suicide) and to concentrate instead on intellectual labors that will honor Hamlet's own life.

A. C. Bradley, one of the most perceptive of Shakespearean critics, compared Hamlet to Brutus and noted that they "are both highly intellectual by nature and reflective by habit. Both may even be called, in a popular sense, philosophic."[25] For Bradley, however, what defines Hamlet are not the external circumstances of the plot or the conscious workings of the prince's mind. The calculating consideration that "cripples the power of acting" of the "thought-sick" prince does not explain to Bradley's satisfaction Hamlet's irresolution. Hamlet's intellectual power is not that of a trained philosopher or artist. Though his learning, however haphazard, comes from his reading, his mind is unrestricted by scholasticism; he is a questioner, a free-thinking critic. According to Bradley, Hamlet "was for ever unmaking his world and rebuilding it in thought, dissolving what to others were solid facts, and discovering what to others were old truths. There were no old truths for Hamlet."[26]

Hamlet's character can be seen from at least two perspectives: his own, that is to say, through his own realization of the manifestations of his melancholic thoughts and doubts and questions; and through the eyes of those around him, friends and foes. From within, Hamlet is an amateur intellectual, a man who is both bewildered and fascinated by the experience of the world but who, instead of performing like a man in the world (according to the Elizabethan notions of masculinity), responds to the world in a womanly fashion, feeling that he "must (like a whore) unpack my heart with words / And fall a-cursing like a very drab, / A scullion!"[27] From without, he is a man aloof (in spite of all his physical demonstrations of action confronting his mother, Ophelia, Polonius, Laertes, even his fellow students, the "tedious old fools"), for reasons of scorn, or madness, or both. Ophelia fears him, Polonius judges him lovesick, Gertrude suspects his mood to stem from her own behavior or from his father's death, Claudius will not allow himself to give a reason for his "distemper." Ophelia sums him up as "a noble mind" and "the courtier's, soldier's, scholar's, eye, tongue, sword," thus combining fine manners, bravery, and intellect "here o'erthrown."[28] Of these three qualities, it is Hamlet's intellect that, from the point of view of his audience, rules him and is at the same time most violently disturbed.

Like Hamlet, Horatio too is a young intellectual (a word that acquires its modern meaning in Shakespeare's time), a student at the University of Wittenberg who, in spite of confessing to a "truant disposition," is undoubtedly a scholar—"friends, scholars and soldiers"[29] Hamlet calls him and Marcellus. Recalling a 1929 production of the play, John Gielgud observed that, in the "moving and convincing" opening scene, the sentinels on the tower, "old and bearded veterans" terrified at the ghost of their old master, showed innocent trust "in the wisdom of the young student Horatio." Horatio "was cleverer than they and would interpret their fears."[30]

Such trust in intellectual power was, in Shakespeare's time as in all ages, not unqualified, and scholars were regarded with a mixture of awe and suspicion. A scholar like Hamlet had no real knowledge of life and yet clung adamantly to his philosophy. Hamlet knows not "seems";[31] "'Sblood," he says of the murky affair, "there is something in this more than natural, if philosophy could find it out."[32] The "if" is rhetorical; Hamlet is convinced that philosophy (or at least, his own philosophical inquiries) *can* find it out.

But in the world of the Danish court, both soldiers and courtiers think of Hamlet as a bookish fop, mouthing the wisdom of his books. Hamlet (like Prospero) is supposed to "know things" only because of his books, and if deprived of these magic amulets, he would lack his vaunted superhuman powers. "Remember," says Caliban to the sailors, trying to convince them to murder the scholarly Prospero, "First to possess his books, for without them / He's but a sot, as I am."[33]

Shakespeare's world was not kind to intellectuals. Though we may like to imagine Shakespeare on the side of Prospero against the brutish Caliban, as we like to imagine him siding with the Prince of Denmark against his murderous uncle, Shakespeare was not an absolute defender of the cloistered reader. True, an Elizabethan playwright was assumed to possess a certain scholarly learning: Nashe ridiculed the "rude upstart" (probably Thomas Kyd) "who never attended university but still had the impudence to set himself up as a playwright."[34] Intellectual pursuits for their own sake are praised ironically in Shakespeare's plays, from the pompous shallows of Jaques's rhetoric or from the heights of Sir Nathaniel's dismissive haughtiness when criticizing poor Dull to the pedant Holofernes: "Sir, he hath never fed on the dainties that are bred in a book; he hath not eat paper, as it were; he hath not drunk ink: his intellect is not replenished; he is only an animal, only sensible in the duller parts."[35]

Arden is all well and good, and Rosalind and Orlando can play their games there, but it is in Duke Frederick's court that true power is held and the course of things determined. Prospero is master of dreams and spirits on his island, protected and guided by his reading, but the reality is that he's a deposed governor, leading an imaginary life in exile. And Hamlet, the studious prince, is the outsider in the tangled web of Denmark's politics, whom King Claudius (for whatever private reasons) wants to force into action, to break his passive disposition and "expel / This something-settled matter in his heart." In fact, Hamlet and his college friends either act wrongly or do not act at all. The example of getting down to business is given by Claudius, or Gertrude, or by the King's ghost, or even by the pompous Polonius, while Hamlet and his comrades are, in the less noble sense, men of words.

Laertes is another matter. He stands somewhere between, neither an active character in any full sense (for all his jumping into graves and unsheathing of swords) nor a dithering literary gentleman (for all his outraged rhetoric). Laertes serves, on the one hand, as a board on which his father Polonius can sound his advice for getting on in the world, for being a man of proper action. On the other hand, Laertes is a mirror for Hamlet and his doubts. "Show me what thou'lt do!"[36] Hamlet shouts at him, although (as Northrop Frye pointed out) "there is nothing appropriate for Laertes to do at this point except kill Hamlet."[37] Laertes is a man of little action and few words.

In the High Middle Ages, the man of words (meaning the scholar of Scripture) was praised as a man of virtue. Thomas Aquinas noted that "according to Augustine in *On Christian Doctrine* 4:12, one skilled in words should so speak as to teach, to delight and to change; that is, to teach the ignorant, to delight the bored and to change the lazy."[38] Augustine had argued that words offered us the possibility of higher understanding by means of what memory could cull from the texts that had been studied. Reading, above all other activities, allowed for a space in which the mind could detach itself from its quotidian surroundings and dwell on loftier matters, not consciously decoding the text on the page but rather allowing the text to transport the reader on an inward journey. Though Augustine believed that only with the resurrection of the body could a state of ultimate bliss be achieved, *something* like that state was possible for the earthly traveler, a moment of illumination granted by the act of reading. For Augustine, reading and writing were divine gifts or obligations imposed upon Adam and Eve for their first disobedience. Before the Fall, they communicated without language, from soul to soul, and after the last trumpet, when language once again would be no longer necessary, reading and writing would vanish from the earth.[39] But while we are of this world, words remain our only, necessary and humble, inheritance.

Therefore, according to Augustine, positive action in this world could be effected through reading, through the passing from the words on the page to thought and to the realm beyond thought, to understanding the evidence of things unseen. The meditative life was the better life, as Christ himself had pointed out to Mary and Martha. To his fellow students Rosencrantz and Guildenstern, Hamlet argues that only thought defines the world, lending it understanding. For Hamlet, being in Denmark stifles his ability to think freely; not so for Guildenstern and Rosencrantz, who enjoy their status as guests of the crown. "Why, then 'tis none to you," Hamlet answers, "for there is nothing either good or bad but thinking makes it so. To me it is a prison."[40] Such nihilism, to use an anachronistic term, was scorned by Shakespeare, for whom the world, as his writing shows, is of unimpeachable reality not dependent on the whims of philosophical lucubration. Things may seem (do seem) one way or another, but blood and stone and human passions and the world itself have a solid existence that (to follow Augustine's story) we have been condemned to translate into words, in a pathetic attempt to apprehend them.

It was Coleridge who began the tradition of seeing Hamlet as a man "paralyzed by excess of thought." According to Coleridge, in the student prince, Shakespeare

seems to have wished to exemplify the moral necessity of a due balance between our attention to the objects of our senses, and our meditation on the workings of our minds,—an *equilibrium* between the real and the imaginary worlds. In Hamlet, this balance is disturbed: his thoughts, and the images of his fancy, are far more vivid than his actual perceptions, and his very perceptions, instantly passing through the *medium* of his contemplations, acquire, as they pass, a form and a colour not naturally their own. Hence we see a great, an almost enormous, intellectual activity, and a proportionate aversion to real action consequent upon it, with all its symptoms and accompanying qualities. This character Shakespeare places in circumstances, under which it is obliged to act on the spur of the moment: Hamlet is brave and careless of death; but he vacillates from sensibility, and procrastinates from thought, and loses the power of action in the energy of resolve.[41]

Hamlet has been warned of the consequences of allowing thought to override action. His father's ghost (which Jacques Derrida cannily defined as "this non-present present, this being-there of an absent which defies semantics as much as ontology, psychoanalysis as much as philosophy") is the paradoxical reminder that "there are more things in heaven and earth"[42] than are dreamed in both Horatio's and Hamlet's philosophy. The ghost is the incarnation of unreal reality, of that which lies beyond the margins of Hamlet's books. To experience it (the ghost is referred to as a thing, not a person), Hamlet must pass from the concreteness of printed words to the evanescent evidence offered by the world. Were Hamlet not to act, the ghost tells him, he'd be duller "than the fat weed / That rots itself in ease on Lethe wharf." Lethe, the river of Hades that offers oblivion, was for the ancients a necessary passage for the souls before their reincarnation.[43] In order for him to act in the world, Lethe must cleanse Hamlet of his intellectual impediments. To learn something new—decisive action—something old must be forgotten, the earlier philosophy must be purged. This is something that Augustine, attempting to reconcile Scripture with his old love of the pagan classics, would have understood well. It is not that Hamlet decides not to act: it is that, stuffed with academic teaching, he will not allow himself to unlearn his university catechism and learn again from the factual experience of what has suddenly broken into his consciousness; that is, the appearance of the ghost that is more than just a nightmarish prodigy in Hamlet's life. As Shakespeare makes clear, it is the beginning of the undermining of Hamlet's entire intellectual universe, of his ethical and moral learning, of his confidence in the reality of what is told in books. As a student, his library was his universe, his entire experience of the world, the world as library which he later sees as a prison. And this may be one of the meanings of his famous utterance:

> I could be bounded in a nutshell,
> And count myself a king of infinite space,
> Were it not that I have bad dreams.[44]

For Hamlet, bounded in his nutshell library, the real world, the world outside books, is an imprisoning nightmare. In this sense, the ghost of Hamlet's father appears as a terrifying liberation. The ghost implicitly demands that Hamlet close his books, step out of the confining space of words and face the painful facts, which, like that of his "too, too solid flesh," refuse to melt. Hamlet (the ghost tells him) must remember his father, the murdered king, and not the "baser matter" written in his books. Thus Hamlet is brutally confronted with a reality (or rather with an "unreality" that is more real than real) that replaces the "trivial fond records" he has chosen to copy down, a worldly reality that overrides the wordy lessons of his books and "tables." These "tables" were habitually kept by students in Shakespeare's time, commonplace books in which they were supposed to copy out inspiring examples and moral teachings from the classics. These must now be replaced by the bloody teachings of his father's ghost. "Remember thee?" Hamlet asks in response to the ghost's injunction,

> Yea, from the table of my memory
> I'll wipe away all trivial fond records,
> All saws of books, all forms, all pressures past
> That youth and observation copied there,
> And thy commandment all alone shall live
> Within the book and volume of my brain,
> Unmixed with baser matter.[45]

Faced with the ghost and its explicit revelations, Hamlet realizes that he must descend from his ivory tower and act. But how should he act? Why is his behavior so puzzling to the other members of the court, each interpreting the Prince's actions according to his or her gullible or guilty eye? Tom Stoppard, in *Rosencrantz and Guildenstern Are Dead,* has one of his clowns sum up the situation: "Your father, whom you love, dies, you are his heir, you come back and find that hardly was the corpse cold before his young brother popped onto his throne and into his sheets, thereby offending both legal and natural practice. Now why exactly are you behaving in this extraordinary manner?"[46]

In fact, as the audience impatiently realizes, Hamlet is not "behaving" at all. Perhaps Coleridge's accusation of willful procrastination is too strong, but the fact remains that after five long acts and many terrible events, Hamlet still has not relinquished words for action, he has not left his ivory tower for the public forum. He dies, but even that is not a wordless event. At the end of the play, the rest is certainly not silence.

Recently, the critic Stephen Greenblatt summarized the play as "the story of the long interval between the first motion . . . and the acting of the dreadful thing."[47] Reflection presented as action, philosophical doubts considered events, a plot that evolves along that which is not done: these are the characteristics of the intellectual act that allow outsiders to judge the thinker, the scholar, the reader as inefficient and abstracted. Though the play can show the active side of inaction (or rather, of mental action) the actor himself is seen in the negative light of what lies in expectation. Jorge Luis Borges once described the aesthetic fact as "the imminence of a revelation that does not take place." That imminence, that promised revelation, turns the ivory tower into a waiting room, and is, for most of us, unbearable.

The reverse notion, that of the ivory tower as a positive place, is the ideal that the historian Jacques Le Goff saw developing earlier, in the Middle Ages. This was the ideal of Thomas

Aquinas, which led to the foundation of universities and libraries as centers for study, in order, not to escape from the world, but better to reflect upon it. According to Le Goff, when the medieval intellectual began to relinquish the closed-in circles of reading and prayer, and entered the spaces of empirical science and political life outside the university and monastery walls, another group of readers took on the role of secluded scholars. "The humanist is an aristocrat," wrote Le Goff of the new intellectuals of the sixteenth and seventeenth centuries. "At once, the humanist takes on the wit, the spirit as his ensign, even as he languishes over his textbooks and his eloquence smells of the midnight oil. He writes only for initiates. When Erasmus publishes his *Adages*, his friends tell him 'You reveal our mysteries!'"

This intellectual world is that of the student Hamlet and of his friends: the closed academy of mysteries that are not revealed to the uninitiated, the privileged world of grammar and the gown. In Oxford, for example, students and masters claimed the privileges of ecclesiastical jurisdiction, and the chancellor ensured for the university such a position of independence that it was said that "the burghers lived in their own town almost as helots or subjects of a conquering people."[48] (In France things were different, Le Goff notes, since the centers of study never achieved a similar degree of separation from the town, so that when the humanists reached Paris, they taught not at the university but in an elitist institution, the College of Royal Readers, the future Collège de France.) Everywhere in

Europe, the humanists worked in silence, hiding the fact that they worked at all and boasting of their leisure, the *otium* of the ancient Romans. "Do not be ashamed of this illustrious and glorious idleness which great souls have always enjoyed," wrote the fifteenth-century theologian Nicolas de Clamanges to the scholar Jean de Montreuil, praising something akin to melancholy, acedia, sloth. Hamlet believes that this leisure will allow him to be a better man, to reign perhaps one day as king of Denmark, but he finds that the world is nothing like the *hortus conclusus*, the enclosed garden of his library. "How weary, stale, flat, and unprofitable," he says, "Seem to me all the uses of this world! / Fie on't! ah, fie! 'Tis an unweeded garden / That grows to seed; things rank and gross in nature / Possess it merely."[49]

As the Shakespearean scholar Jonathan Bate notes, Shakespeare "has a more practical mind than Prospero [and Hamlet]. His dramatic art translates a theme of ancient books from the *vita contemplativa* to the *vita activa* by virtue of his very medium of production: unlike the private contemplative space of the library, the public sphere of the theatre belongs to the active social life of the citizen. The humanist defense of theatre against Puritanism was that theatre had the capacity to bring to a wider public the kind of moral edification that was available privately and selectively to elite humanist readers by means of their book learning."[50] For Shakespeare, who was not a university man, the concept of the ivory tower from which Hamlet refuses to emerge was one to be scorned.

And yet, as A. D. Nuttall has asserted, "It is hard to think of anything in Hamlet of which one can be finally sure."[51] For the successive generations, Hamlet's refusal proved difficult to accept, perhaps because it reflected other uneasy refusals that his audience was unwilling to recognize. From Coleridge's reading onward, attempts were made to rescue the Prince from his tower, to show that the scornful confinement had not, in fact, fully seduced him.

On 23 April 1940, the German drama critic Wolfgang Keller addressed the German Shakespeare Society with these words: "Outside, in and over the wild North Sea, our brave forces, in fearless vessels or in roaring planes, are attacking the British warships and their hiding places. The British who, allied with our indefatigable enemies in the West, are waging a war of annihilation against us. . . . We, however, celebrate Shakespeare, a son of English soil. But can we?"[52]

Two centuries earlier, Johann Gottfried Herder had noted Shakespeare's roots in Nordic poetry and proposed the idea that, born in England "by mistake," Shakespeare was in fact German. Following on Herder's claim, Keller boasted that Germany had been the first European country to translate Shakespeare (Caspar W. von Borck translated *Julius Caesar* into German in 1741). With this act, Keller argued, the Germans first rose to claim their right to Shakespeare. Furthermore, Keller went on to say, two centuries of German critical work on Shakespeare had given Germany the right to rate "the greatest dramatist of the Germanic tribes as a German classic, which no British policy can ever steal from us." To justify this claim, Keller pointed out the similarities he perceived between Elizabethan England and the Third Reich. "The sense of life of the Elizabethans," Keller wrote, "was heroic, military, young and striving for progress, hungry for actions and adventures." But the reason Germany itself had so far failed to produce a Shakespeare of its own, was clear: Shakespeare's England had been "free of Jews for 300 years."

Hamlet was the Third Reich's favorite Shakespeare play. Between 1936 and 1941, the Berlin Staatstheater staged it almost two hundred times. One of the most noted productions was directed by Lothar Müthel, with the celebrated Gustav Gründgens in the title role. Gründgens was perhaps the most famous actor in German theater history: he became known for playing Mephistopheles in Goethe's *Faust*, and later was the subject of the novel *Mephisto*, in which Gründgens's brother-in-law, Klaus Mann, depicted Gründgens's collaboration with the Nazi regime. Gründgens played Hamlet against the traditional expectations. Instead of the uncertain, reflective intellectual, Gründgens depicted Hamlet as brave and determined, and anything but hesitant. In the words of Gründgens's biographer, Curt Riess: "A new Hamlet is born, one that had not been seen before. A Hamlet full of responsibility, a Hamlet ready to act, and not afraid to play the fool." To achieve this, any lines that suggested passivity were cut, and scene 4 of act IV was deleted in its entirety. For Riess, "other Hamlets could ask themselves whether they should act or not. For Gründgens, there was no such question, as long as the regime of terror existed, as long as criminals ruled." In a startling paradox, the actor with Nazi sympathies depicted his hero as a resister against tyranny, Danish in the text, Nazi in the eyes of a discerning audience. No contemporary costumes were needed to signal the comparison: Gründgens wore a wide-collared cape and a hat with a vertical brim, more a foppish Wittenberg student than a warrior prince. And yet the effect was that of powerful action. "When the curtain rises," Gründgens himself wrote to one of his critics, "I don't want to play Hamlet, I want to go back to Wittenberg. It is against my will that I am burdened with a truth I cannot withdraw from. . . . I want to act but I must know. Otherwise I cannot act." Philosophical reflection is, for Gründgens's Hamlet, not a self-serving indulgence but an intellectual function that leads forcefully to action. In Gründgens's interpretation, the ivory tower becomes not a sanctuary but a watch tower.

The Watch Tower

Let the masses read morals, but for goodness sake
don't give them poetry to spoil.
—Stéphane Mallarmé, *Proses de jeunesse*

The notion of the retiring intellectual was likewise derided, for different reasons and with different arguments, by Marxist thinkers. Antonio Gramsci, more vigorously than others, saw the intellectual's role as the opposite of Hamlet's, not waiting and reflecting, but setting out, exploring and deciphering the intricate problems of society, and having an active hand in the passage from capitalism to socialism, and in the running of a socialist state: not only a revolutionary elite but the whole reading public, consciously exercising its intellectual talents.

Gramsci was deeply interested in the role of the intellectual in society. He attacked the idea of culture as mere encyclopedic knowledge, and saw in the attitude of certain students and pro-

Franz Kafka's drawing of a figure on a balcony.

fessionals an excuse to differentiate themselves hierarchically from the masses. "They end up seeing themselves as different from and superior to even the best skilled workman, who fulfils a precise and indispensable task in life and is a hundred times more valuable in his activity than they are in theirs. But this is not culture, but pedantry, not intelligence, but intellect, and it is absolutely right to react against it."[53] For Gramsci, "all human beings are intellectuals but not all have in society the *function* of intellectuals; that is to say, not everyone has a social intellectual function."[54] Each existing social group creates within itself strata of intellectuals that give it meaning, help to bind it together and help it function: managers, civil servants, the clergy, teachers, scientists, lawyers, doctors, and so on. For Gramsci, the intellectual does not belong to a separate social class but acts within a specific class, according to that class's needs. Thus Hamlet acts within the circles of the intellectual royalty and cannot conduct himself according to the manners of the military aristocracy (like Horatio) or the political bourgeoisie (like Laertes).

In his *Prison Notebooks* Gramsci distinguished between "organic" and "traditional" intellectuals, both seen by society to belong to two distinct categories. The "organic intellectual" seems explicitly to be part of a particular social class, allied to and assisting the ruling class, a product of the official educational system taught to perform a function for the dominant social group. It is through this organic intellectual that the ruling class maintains its hegemony over the rest of society.[55]

Following this definition, the social theorist C. L. R. James observed that in Shakespeare's time "the intellectual was an organic part of rationalist society and Hamlet is the organic intellectual."[56]

The "traditional intellectual," instead, is defined by Gramsci as independent of any specific social class. As literati, religious thinkers, essayists, and poets such as Erasmus and Shakespeare, intellectuals of this sort appear as autonomous and independent individuals, part of a lineage unbroken by strife and social upheaval. In the hands of these was the task of countering the official "common sense." Since for Gramsci "there is no human activity from which every form of intellectual participation can be excluded," it followed that everyone, in some form or another, performs an intellectual activity, "participates in a particular conception of the world, has a conscious line of moral conduct, and therefore contributes to sustain a conception of the world or to modify it, that is, to bring into being new modes of thought."

"Is it better to 'think,'" asked Gramsci, "without having a critical awareness, or is it better to work out consciously and critically one's own conception of the world?" Gramsci's words unconsciously echo Hamlet's more famous question, still unanswered. The verb "to be" carries in English a double meaning, rendered explicit in Spanish, for instance: "ser," meaning to exist, and "estar" meaning to be in a certain manner or place. Gramsci's dichotomy offers Hamlet two distinct possibilities: to reside in his library tower, as a reader for whom the limits of his reading coincide with the margins of his books; or to take his reading out into the open, to confront the book in his hands with the book of the world, as Augustine suggested.

At the beginning of one of his posthumously published notebooks, Franz Kafka wrote: "Every person carries a room inside himself."[57] That room, which Democritus and the Christian hermits, Montaigne, and Virginia Woolf externalized, others, such as Hamlet, never fully left. Here the world played itself out for private contemplation, allowing itself to be rebuilt according to the sitter's pleasure, imagination, ambition, patience, will.

In Shakespeare's time, the yet unnamed ivory tower, praised as a sanctuary (albeit fraught with danger) by the scholars of the Middle Ages, was commonly derided as a refuge for cowards. Centuries later, after Sainte-Beuve had invoked it to praise the poetic craft that deals only with inspired words, the ivory tower became once again an object of ridicule, the egotistical choice of inaction over action, which neither the Third Reich's attempt at recuperation nor Gramsci's inspired call to intellectual arms was entirely successful in overturning.

Today, the reader in the ivory tower has become emblematic of yet another position. At a time when the values that our societies put forward as desirable are those of speed and brevity, the slow, intense, reflective process of reading is seen as inefficient and old-fashioned. Electronic reading of various kinds does not seem to encourage prolonged sessions with a single text but rather to encourage a pecking process of short fragments. Communications historian Nicholas Carr, in *The*

Shallows, speaks of certain digital-media scholars who suggest that "we shouldn't waste our time mourning the death of deep reading—it was overrated all along," and who went on to judge *War and Peace* and *In Search of Lost Time* as "too long and not so interesting." While not taking these postures too seriously, Carr identifies such declarations as important signs of the shift that is taking place in society's attitude toward intellectual achievement. "Their words," says Carr, "make it a lot easier for people to justify that shift—to convince themselves that surfing the Web is a suitable, even superior substitute for deep reading and other forms of calm and attentive thought. In arguing that books are archaic and dispensable, [these critics] provide the intellectual cover that allows thoughtful people to slip comfortably into the permanent state of distractedness that defines the online life."[58] In fact, to bind themselves in nutshells, and count themselves kings of infinite space.

CHAPTER 3

THE BOOKWORM

The Reader as Inventor of the World

"Now I declare that's too bad!" Humpty
Dumpty cried, breaking into a sudden passion.
"You've been listening at doors—and behind
trees—and down chimneys—or you couldn't
have known it!"

"I haven't, indeed!" Alice said very gently.
"It's in a book."

—Lewis Carroll,
Through the Looking-Glass, Chapter VI

The Creature Made of Books

I have sought for happiness everywhere, but I have
found it nowhere except in a little corner with a book.

—Thomas à Kempis

At a table made of huge books laid flat and borne on legs of
parchment scrolls, a wizened man with large spectacles turns
the leaves of a thick book with his chin. He cannot use his
hands: his body is cocooned in a sheaf of printed paper, poised

on an open treatise. The back wall is covered with huge pages and a shelf full of books. He is the bookworm, mocked in an 1842 caricature by the French cartoonist Jean Ignace Isidore Gérard, known as Grandville. The meaning of the jest is clear: here is someone literally made out of print, so absorbed in the words on the page that nothing else seems to exist for him. In his book-centered world, the flesh has become the word.

Does this metamorphosis grant him special powers? According to Grandville, it would not seem so. All the reader can do, bound by his strange fate, is peruse with his eyes the book in front of him, page after page; he is helpless in every other sense. He has no effect on the world around him: even his own body, swathed in paper, seems not his to command. And though his cocoon-like appearance suggests that a butterfly might be born from his captive state, no indication is given of when, if ever, this rebirth is likely to happen. In Grandville's depiction, the bookworm seems condemned to his cloistered fate for as long as there are books to be read.

Though this caricature of the reader's fate illustrates the negative aspects of the ivory tower, it is not, thankfully, the overriding image of the reader in our world. Images of readers in every conceivable situation have been produced since our earliest literate civilizations, endowed with complex symbolic meanings of identity, power, and privilege. Whether hold-

J. J. Grandville, "A bookworm." From *Vies Publiques et Privées des Animaux* (1840–1842). Courtesy the Granger Collection, New York.

ing in their hands something sacred, something dangerous, something instructive or entertaining, whether dipping into a trove of memory and learning, whether listening to the voice of their contemporaries or ancestors, to the Word of God or the words of those long dead, readers are depicted as engaging in a mysterious, numinous act. Implicit in the act are the reader's capacities: to rescue experience, transgress physical laws, translate and reinterpret information, learn facts, delight in lies, and judge.

Also implicit are the rules by which the reader engages with the writer, establishing territories of responsibility and obligation, as well as borders that must not be transgressed, unless by an act of subversion on either side. Depending on what the text is supposed to be, on its agreed-upon identity, reader and writer have different duties and expectations. According to convention, fiction demands one set of rules, biography another, and generations of readers and writers have endeavored to break, undermine, and renew these basic preconceptions.

Three centuries before Grandville, the scholar Nicholas de Herberay prefaced his translation into French of the first volume of the chivalry romance *Amadís de Gaula* with a sonnet in which he asks the readers to content themselves with the story the writer has presented for them, and not inquire about its truth.

Kind reader, with keen judgment gifted,
When you discover the refined invention

Of this author, be with the style content

And ask not if what takes place is true.[1]

It is a curious invocation. To warn the reader not to compare too closely the facts of the books with the facts of reality carries the implicit acknowledgment of textual untruth, transgressing the rules by which both reader and author agree to undertake the romance, the former suspending disbelief, the latter lending verisimilitude to the story.

The contract that writer and reader enter when the one closes the book and the other opens it is a contract of self-deception and mutual pretense, in which limits are set to dismissive skepticism and unbridled trust, establishing what Umberto Eco called "the limits of interpretation."[2] There is, lurking at the core of every reader's engagement with the text, a double bind: the wish that what is told on the page be true, and the belief that it is not. In this tension between both, readers set up their tenuous encampment. Bruno Bettelheim long ago noted that children do not believe in the Big Bad Wolf or in Little Red-Riding Hood as such: they believe in their narrative existence, which, as we all know, can have a greater hold on us than many characters of blood and bone.[3] For most readers, however, engagement with a text does not go beyond passionate daydreaming or wishful thinking.

And yet, there are readers for whom the world on the page acquires such vividness, such truth, that it overrides the world of the rational senses. Outside clinical cases, every reader has felt, at least once, the overwhelming power of a creature of words, falling in love with a certain character, viscerally loathing another, hoping to emulate a third. Saint Augustine tells us that, in his youth, he wept for the death of Dido. Robert Louis Stevenson's neighbors in Samoa begged him to show them the bottle containing the evil imp. And still today the London Post Office sorts letters addressed to Mr. Sherlock Holmes at 221B Baker Street.

With such raptures in mind, readers have often been portrayed as prey to these imaginary beings, as victims of unreal happenings, as devourers of books who are, in turn, themselves devoured by literary monsters. Seen from the perspective of those who do not read or inordinately care for books, the passionate engagement with the page seems vacuous and unhealthy, resulting, as in Grandville's cartoon, in a creature not of flesh and blood but of paper and ink. Every reader, past and present, has at least once heard the injunction: "Stop reading! Go out and live!"—as if reading and life were two separate states of being, as if the admonisher feared that the reader might no longer know the difference between what is solid flesh and what is not. The Book Fool, a figure who first appears as such in the sixteenth century, in Sebastian Brant's *Ship of Fools*, is the incarnation of this ubiquitous reproach. Whether skimming through his books in a belled fool's cap (as in Albrecht Dürer's illustration to Brant's book), or in the guise of a studious donkey (in Olearius's satire *De fide concubinarum* of 1505), or as a librarian occupied only with the dust gathered

on books (in Abraham a Sancta Clara's *Hundred Distinguished Fools* of 1709), the Book Fool became an established icon of the literary world.

The Book Fool is, among other things, the omnivorous reader who mistakes accumulation of books for the acquisition of knowledge, and who ends up convinced that the events narrated between covers are the events of the real world. He or she: here the humanists were disposed to include both sexes. Erasmus, in his *Praise of Folly*, taking his cue from the Book of Proverbs, depicted the Book Fool as female. "If it should happen that a woman should wish to appear wise, she will only succeed in being twice as foolish," Erasmus wrote. "Because a vice is doubled when it is disguised as virtue, going against

"The Book Fool." From Sebastian Brant, *The ship of fooles: wherein is shewed the folly of all states,* trans. Alexander Barclay Priest (London: Iohn Cavvood, 1570). Courtesy the University of Pennsylvania Rare Book and Manuscript Library.

nature and all innate tendencies. . . . A woman is always a woman: that is to say, a fool."[4]

The Book Fools are the women and men who "love all devouring words" (as the psalmist has it), and devour in turn volume after volume, but are (again, according to the psalmist) "like a broken vessel" because they cannot retain instruction. In most cultures of the written word, they have been compared to one of those small,

A teaching ass. From Paul Olearius [Jacob Wimpfeling],
De fide concubinarum in sacerdotes (1505).

hungry creatures who have, since before the days of Alexandria, been the scavengers of libraries: in Spanish, mice, in German and French, rats, in English, worms, after the *Anobium pertinax*. The actual bookworm (the larva of the *Anobium*) was first described by Richard Hooke in 1665, who compared its voracious, elongated form to "one of the teeth of Time."[5] An Anglo-Saxon riddle from the ninth century describes the creature's habits:

Johann Christoph Weigel, "Book Fool."
From Abraham a Sancta Clara, *Centi-folium stultorum* (Nuremberg: Weigel, 1709).

A worm had swallowed some man's lay, a thief
In darkness had consumed the mighty saying
With its foundation firm. The thief was not
One whit wiser when he ate those words.[6]

Probably an imitation of an earlier Latin poem, the Anglo-Saxon riddle makes explicit the voracious reader's fault: to swallow the words without benefiting from the meaning, translating the text not into grounded experience but into wishful thinking. The bookworm, in spite of all the devoured books, remains a fool.

No doubt behind this depiction lies a deep, dark unease: the mistrust societies have always had toward that which can be created out of words, a mistrust of the intellectual act itself. This mistrust, this superstitious fear, is perhaps born from the fact that in a number of mythologies the world is created through an utterance, so that words, or the Word, give birth to the universe and to everything in it. Fear of the word can therefore be understood as fear of the magical power of words, and it is tempting to see in most textual censorships, book burnings, mockeries of the reader's craft, an exorcising attempt to defeat the suspected wizardry of language itself.

Robert Hooke, "A bookworm." From *Micrographia, or, Some physiological descriptions of minute bodies made by magnifying glasses: with observations and inquiries thereupon* (London: Jo. Martyn and Ja. Allestry, 1665). Courtesy the University of Pennsylvania Rare Book and Manuscript Library.

It may be that a society, defining itself through the erecting of walls, nurtures at the same time the suspicion that within those walls something will be born that will contest its definition, will seek to alter its identity. And even though our societies grow in the give-and-take between that which we exclude and that which we include, we are more wary of the critical and inventive force of language than we are proud of its power to preserve. Consequently, we attempt to restrict or deride its imaginative efforts.

Exemplary in this sense is the very first scene of Stendhal's *Le Rouge et le noir*. Julian's father, seeing his son reading instead of tending to the mill, tears the book out of the boy's hands and flings it into the river. Similar scenes are repeated in a number of novels and biographies, from the life of Jean Racine to Roald Dahl's *Matilda*, and have become emblematic of society's attitude toward the reader. Since the days of the Mesopotamian and Egyptian scriptoria, the reader's craft has been suspected of being magically dangerous. Anachronistically, we might ask whether there was an implied Book Fool mockery in the Egyptian representation of the god of scribes as a baboon.

In the late Middle Ages and Renaissance, the identity of the Book Fool was created to deride and undermine certain aspects of the reader's power. His features were exaggerated, his attitude ridiculed, in order to associate him, not with the wise fool, not with "Christ's Fool" described by Saint Paul in his First Letter to the Corinthians,[7] but with the "sot" of popular stories and plays, the dullard, the ignoramus who, like the worm, devours books but remains foolish.

The distinction between the serious reader, the scholar, and the mere devourer of books is of the essence. Already in the sixth century, Boethius, in his *Consolation of Philosophy*, made a clear distinction between the Book Fool and the serious reader. When Lady Philosophy appears to him in a vision, as he sits sick and despondent in his prison cell, she insists that the Muses of Poetry who have been inspiring him (and whom she calls "scenicas meretriculas," or, as David Slavitt freely translates it, "chorus girls")[8] should leave immediately, since they have nothing to offer a scholarly mind. "Now, were it some common man whom your allurements were seducing, as is usually your way, I should be less indignant. On such a one I should not have spent my pains for naught. But this is one nurtured in the Eleatic and Academic philosophies. Nay, get ye gone, ye sirens, whose sweetness lasteth not; leave him for my muses to tend and heal!"[9]

The Muses of Poetry (or the Muses of Bestsellerdom, we might say today) stuff the boorish reader with foolishness; the Muses of Philosophy nourish the inspired reader with healing fodder for the soul. These two opposing notions of how we ingest a text derive, as we have seen, from the Book of Ezekiel[10] and the Apocalypse. When Saint John is commanded to "take it, and eat it up," he tells us that "It was in my mouth sweet as honey and as soon as I had eaten it, my belly was bitter."[11] Because he has eaten the Holy Book, Saint John must now go beyond the delicious taste of his reading; he must profit from the text's bitter learning and go out and "prophesy again before many peoples, and nations, and tongues, and kings." As wise readers know, eating the book eventually leads to speaking the book.

Eventually, the distinction between the gluttonous and the ruminating reader, both of whom obediently "ate" words, became unclear, and the depiction of the indiscriminating Book Fool came to overshadow that of his wise counterpart and stand for any reader. Even if Sebastian Brant and his fellow humanists understood and insisted on the differences between ingesting carefully and indiscriminate snacking, between reading in depth and superficial reading, the powerful image that served as frontispiece to *The Ship of Fools* imposed itself almost everywhere.

Still today, glasses are the emblem of the egghead, of the nonsexual being. Dorothy Parker's ditty is still rooted in the popular imagination:

Men seldom make passes
At girls who wear glasses.

Marilyn Monroe echoed this in *How to Marry a Millionaire*, where she refused to wear glasses in order to find a husband. Or, in the male version, Tony Curtis, in *Some Like It Hot*, did wear glasses so that Marilyn would believe that he had no sexual drive—a Book Fool indeed.

Eventually, the Book Fool acquired all the negative connotations that society projected onto the reader: a creature lost in a wilderness of words, with no hold on everyday reality, living in a world of make-believe that is of no practical use to his fellow citizens. "Why read the *Princesse de Clèves*?" asked the president of France, Nicolas Sarkozy, in 2009 on discovering that civil servants were meant to study this classic seventeenth-century novel for their entrance exams.[12] What he meant was: how can reading fiction possibly help an administrator of the Republic, someone commissioned to deal with facts and figures and the serious reality of politics? Hélène Cixous wisely asked: "Why this fury against French language and literature? This resentment? This frenzy? Because here is a world on which he cannot pull the old trick of the law of the strongest. He doesn't know how to seduce thought, how to reduce it, dominate it, make it crawl."[13] This is the resentment of many of those in power, those who oppose political and economic forces to intellectual drive, and find that they cannot eliminate the human capacity to imagine the world through language. For this very reason, Plato would banish poets from his ideal Republic: because poets make things up in order to understand the world, they deal with images of reality, not with incomprehensible reality itself.

These negative qualities associated with the reader as Book Fool extended also to the book itself. In the early Middle Ages, the book, as object, could elicit reverence and even fear. It appears enthroned as God's Word in numerous representations:

both as the roll, the *rotulus* or *volumen*, representing the laws of the Old Testament, and as the codex, representing the laws of the New. Gradually, the notions of old and new, applied to containers of the text, acquired connotations of value. Contaminated perhaps by a false etymology, *rotulus* and *volumen* became pejorative words. *Rotulus* evoked not only what was old but also what was "deceitful," "rolled up upon itself," "coiled like a worm" (as in Grandville's depiction).[14] And *volumen* was mistakenly associated with *vulpes* or *volpes*, the fox, which medieval bestiaries explained was called *volpes* because it walked "with its paws turned backwards," "volvere pedibus," a sure sign of its treacherous nature.[15]

The codex, however, depending on whether it was represented as open or as closed (and in what manner opened or closed) could carry either a positive or a negative value. For instance, the lion of Saint Mark, the ubiquitous beast chosen as the emblem of Venice, was represented, from the last decades of the thirteenth century onward, either as a positive emblem, with an open book displaying the words with which the angel announced to the Evangelist that Venice would be his final resting place, or as a negative one, with a closed book to signal a time of war or pestilence. The variations on these symbols are many. The open book displayed by the lion in times of peace and prosperity suggested that the activity of reading was one of leisure, a becoming and scholarly occupation, part of cultured *otium* (Hamlet's studious melancholy) as opposed to the business of state. Or it may be seen as a warning, reminding readers that the Word of God, like his eye, is always watching, threatening to withdraw the present moment of grace. During evil times, the closed book might have meant that once grace was withdrawn, comfort was no longer offered. Now it was too late to read, study, learn. The community of readers should have acted better on their acquired wisdom, descended from their respective towers, and instructed the unlettered how to live harmoniously. *War is no time for books*, the lion and his closed volume seemed to say. *We will return to the sanity of words when the madness is over.*

The Bewitched Reader

Here Doctor, cry'd she, pray sprinkle every Creek and
Corner of this Room, lest there should lurk in it some
one of the many Sorcerers these Books swarm with,
who might chance to bewitch us.
                    —Miguel de Cervantes, *Don Quixote*, I:6

Like the Venetian lion caught between the prestige of intellectual power and mockery at the inefficiency of words, the reader

Francisco Goya, "Don Quixote" (c. 1812–1820). British Museum, London.
Courtesy Alinari / Art Resource, NY.

became trapped in a double bind. The book lover became the Book Fool, and the devourer of books became the bookworm, both parodies of the enraptured reader. "In short, he became so immersed in his books that he spent the night reading from dusk to dawn, and the days from dawn to dusk, until at last, from little sleeping and much reading, his brain dried up, and he came to lose his wits." This is how, in 1605, Cervantes defined the Book Fool we know as Don Quixote. And yet, when Cervantes portrayed his brave knight, he was not quite defining the reader rendered mad by his books. Rather, Cervantes was defining a society madly afraid of its own untruths. No doubt, as we are told in the opening chapter, Alonso Quijano believes in the factual reality of the stories he reads. But then, throughout the novel, it becomes clear that Don Quixote's conception of the world is something more complex than mere delusion. On several occasions, on the verge of allowing himself to be swept away by the fantasy concocted from his readings, Don Quixote negotiates the chasm between what is real in the world and what is real to his imagination, with lucid intuition. Many times he allows the fantasy to overwhelm him, as in the famous scene of the windmills, and suffers the consequences with his battered bones. But at other times he enters the fantasy consciously, like a reader who knows that the story is fiction and yet believes in its revealed truth, as when Don Quixote forbids Sancho to peep under the blindfold and see whether or not the wooden horse is truly carrying them through the skies; or when the enamored knight refuses to show the muleteers a portrait of Dulcinea as proof that she is the most beautiful woman on earth, "for what good would it be to swear, if you need proof in reality."

In counterpoint, neither is the hold of the "real" world all that strong on those who deem the knight to be mad. The curate and the barber, who cull Don Quixote's library in order to rid it of "pernicious" titles, preserve however from the flames a fair number of volumes that they believe to be important (for themselves) both as entertainment and as means of knowledge. The innkeeper who holds public readings of novels of chivalry tells how for each of his listeners—reapers, farmhands, prostitutes, youngsters—the story acquires a personal meaning and gives a private delight, helping them bear the hardships and sorrows of daily life. And the aristocrats who make fun of the poor old knight and play cruel jokes on him live in a world in which they transform their fantasies into realities and their whims into a parody of justice. This play between the explicit imaginary world of the protagonist and the unconscious world of those around him places the reader of *Don Quixote* uncertainly between both, as one of the solitary creatures who find in books the experience of reality, and also as a member of the society that derides reading and wishes to impose its own views of what is and is not collectively worthy.

In Plato's seventh (and perhaps apocryphal) letter, the philosopher states that there are certain truths that cannot be put into writing. And even if they can be written of, they cannot not be learned by merely perusing the page: they must be discovered by the readers themselves after much toil and experience, when suddenly the knowledge springs like a spark into the soul, allowing it to feed itself.[16] This argument, repeated over the centuries, suggests that reading cannot teach us the truest, deepest things, and that to pretend to supplant life with reading is folly.

And yet, putting into writing words that describe experience has a prestige far greater than that of intuitive learning. In the early fourteenth century, Rabbi Sem Tob de Carrión, in his *Moral Proverbs*, noted what was by then a commonplace:

> The word pronounced / is by and by forgotten,
> But writing remains / for ever preserved.
> And the arguments not / set down in writing,
> Are like arrows / that will not reach their goal.[17]

In spite of Plato's warning, writing (and therefore reading) became a means of instruction and knowledge. Even if the reader knew that the stories were made up and the characters only lived in the imagination of their author, this stuff made of dreams acted upon the minds of readers as models of the world in which we still attempt to survive.

"As manifest experience shows, the weakness of memory, consigning to oblivion not only those deeds made old by time but also the fresh events of our own era, has made it appropriate, useful, and expedient to record in writing the feats of strong and courageous men of old. Such men are the brightest of mirrors, examples and sources of righteous instruction, as we are told by the noble orator Tully."[18] Thus begins *Tirant lo Blanc*, the novel of chivalry that the barber and the priest, intent on burning Don Quixote's library, decide to save from the bonfire as "the best book of its kind in the world."[19] Even within a story that appears to condemn the reading of such books as folly, it is stated that certain of these books lead us to the contrary of folly, and grant us "mirrors, examples and sources" of ancient righteousness and illustrious behavior.

CONCLUSION

READING TO LIVE

People say that life's the thing, but I prefer reading.
—Logan Pearsall Smith, *Afterthoughts*

Two and a half centuries after the publication of the first part of *Don Quixote*, Gustave Flaubert pursued the exploration of the reader as mediator between the perception of fiction and the perception of reality. The reader as traveler, the reader in the ivory tower, the reader as devourer of books, all appear in Flaubert's works from his very earliest writings. The reader as life's apprentice lies at the core of all Flaubert's books.

Flaubert regarded himself as a reader-traveler, and the books he read as a cartography that helped him explore the world of experience. "Read to live!"[1] is his famous advice to his friend, Mademoiselle de Chantepie. His last book, *Bouvard and Pécuchet*, portrays two bookish fools who believe that by reading everything they will acquire, as travelers of the printed page,

Bernard Naudin, "Bouvard and Pécuchet."
From *Oeuvres complètes illustrées de Gustave Flaubert* (Paris: Librairie de France, 1923).

full knowledge of the world. But the novel, left unfinished at his death, cannot reach a conclusion: there is no last page either to Bouvard and Pécuchet's endeavor or to the chronicle of their efforts penned by Flaubert. Unlike Dante's travels that end in the ineffable, the journey of Flaubert's two book fools never comes to the final line of the countless books that they could read, and therefore never reaches the Dantesque revelation that cannot be put into words. Their journey is, as it were, the down-to-earth version of Dante's otherworldly pilgrimage, a heroic attempt to do the seemingly impossible, knowing that it is impossible and that it must fail.

And yet, in spite of such heroic failures, Flaubert believed that books allowed a reader (the wise reader, not the Book Fool) a sane sanctuary for thought. Rejoining Hamlet, Flaubert defined the ivory tower as a refuge against the world's imbecility, a place where a reader can be at peace with the intelligence of his books even though these be made up of "words, words, words." In another letter to Mademoiselle de Chantepie, dated Tuesday, 23 January 1866, Flaubert pities her for having to bear the "fanaticism and stupidity" of the province (Mademoiselle de Chantepie was then living in Angers): "When people no longer believe in the Immaculate Conception, they'll believe in ouija boards. We must find consolation in this and go live in an ivory tower. It's not fun, I know, but if one follows this method, one is neither a gullible fool nor a charlatan."[2] This is Flaubert's tongue-in-cheek take on Horace's *beatus ille*, the classic praise of those who withdraw from the throng of city business to the studious peace of the country. For Flaubert both city and country were contaminated, the former by bourgeois conventionality, the latter by peasant doltishness. The ivory tower was the only refuge for a sane person seeking to escape the world's stupidity. Bouvard and Pécuchet never truly find their ivory tower.

Bouvard and Pécuchet was Flaubert's last work; the short story "Bibliomania" was his first, published in 1837, when Flaubert was sixteen years old. It tells of an antiquarian bookseller so passionate about collecting books that he will even commit murder to obtain one. "He loved a book because it was a book," Flaubert says of him. "He loved its smell, its shape, its title." To which Flaubert added: "He could barely read."[3] The obsessive bibliomaniac is one of the deadlier incarnations of the bookworm who accumulates books without traveling through them, without reading them in studious seclusion, without making them truly his. He is the hoarder of dead symbols, unwilling or unable to breathe life into the book, since it is the reader's breath (his incarnate reading, as Saint Augustine argued) that gives the book life.

The same year he published "Bibliomania" Flaubert wrote another story, "Passion and Virtue," "a philosophical tale" (as he called it) whose plot he had found in the law courts' gazetteer, concerning the adultery and consequent suicide of a health official's wife. In this adolescent tale, the heroine is not explicitly a bookworm, and yet the world of romantic fiction is clearly present in her dreams, her conversations, her ideas of what love should and should not be. Years later, the health official's wife would be reincarnated in a clearer version of the bookworm, the romantically obsessed Emma Bovary.

Flaubert's three bookish Bs (the bibliomaniac, Bouvard, and Bovary) are all Book Fools with one common ancestor. Writing to his lover, Louise Colet, on 12 June 1852, almost ten months after having begun *Madame Bovary*, Flaubert confessed to her that all his roots were to be found "in the book I knew by heart before knowing how to read, *Don Quixote*" (overlaid, he added, with "the agitated foam of the seas of Normandy, the English sickness [epilepsy], and the stinking fog").[4] *Don Quixote* was to provide Flaubert with the uneasy model of a fiction in which "art"—meaning "that which is artificial or stylish"—seemed to Flaubert happily absent.[5] Because even in apparently "artificial" works such as *The Temptation of St. Anthony* or *Salammbô*, absence of artificiality was to Flaubert of the essence. At ten in the morning, on 4 May 1880, in a letter addressed to Guy de Maupassant, Flaubert wrote: "The importance attached to foolishness, and pedantic futility exasperate me! Bafouons le chic!" ("Let us scorn stylishness!").[6] These were Flaubert's last penned words. Four days after writing them he died.

In *Madame Bovary*, the pretentious pharmacist Homais is attracted to that futility which Flaubert derided. "What seduced him above all was the chic."[7] Chic—stylishness, not style. And it is also this chic, this stylishness, that seduces Emma as a reader, a chic that she mistakes for elegance. What Emma finds in her romantic books is a contrast to the tedium, the inaneness, the dreariness of her life with Charles Bovary—no matter how badly the books are written, no matter how artificial the language used. It is the passionate chic adventures that matter to her, because, unlike Don Quixote, who can (when necessary) distinguish between what is real and what is fiction, Emma when reading her books translates their romantic plots straight into the world of her own desires.

Emma's first books are small, gaudily bound volumes received as school prizes, which she proudly shows Charles during their first meetings. Later come the novels in which she will find enhanced versions of her affair with the viscount: she reads books by Eugène Sue, Balzac, George Sand, "seeking imaginary satisfaction for her private desires. . . . The memory of the viscount would constantly return in her reading. Between him and the imaginary characters she would establish links. But the circle of which he was the centre gradually became larger around him, and the halo he possessed, spreading out from his image, stretched out far away, illuminating other dreams."[8]

"Imaginary satisfaction for her private desires": Emma's readings color her entire world. They are her history, her geography, her spiritual mirror. So caught up is she in the fictional world, she even brings her books to the dinner table, turning the leaves while her husband tries to speak to her, telling her stories from his working day. Emma responds to these attempts with passionate scenes from her novels. Because having transformed herself into an emblematic bookworm, books are now her food, the stuff on which her world is built.

A. S. Byatt, recalling her first encounter with *Madame Bovary*, noted that what makes it impossible for Emma "to inhabit her house or her marriage is her romantic sense that there is something more, some more intense experience, some wider horizon if she could only find it. Her desires are formed by her reading and her education."[9] When reality fails to live up to her fiction, Emma blames her books. "I've read everything," she says, anticipating Mallarmé. In the end, Emma will attempt suicide because life is dreary and books no longer offer consolation. Having served as fodder for her dreams rather than proper nourishment for the soul, books can now neither encourage nor satisfy her. For Emma, both on the page and in the world, there is, in the end, no "wider horizon." Like the bookworm in the Anglo-Saxon riddle, she has not truly benefited from the books she has devoured.

After Cervantes, the readers in fiction (that is to say, fictional characters who are both the subject and the object of a novel) become more literally conscious of the gastronomy of reading. From Arabella, in Charlotte Lennox's slightly silly eighteenth-century romp, *The Female Quixote*, in which the heroine forces the world around her to mirror the romantic novels that delight her, "supposing romances were real pictures of life,"[10] to Tolstoy's Anna Karenina, for whom reading is a taunting reminder of the life not lived, fiction makes its exemplary role explicit.

After Anna Karenina's meeting with Vronsky in Moscow, she returns to St. Petersburg. On the train she picks up a book and a paper-knife to cut the pages, and reads. "Anna read and understood, but it was unpleasant for her to read, that is, to follow the reflection of other people's lives. She wanted too much to live herself. When she read about the heroine of the novel taking care of a sick man, she wanted to walk with inaudible steps around the sick man's room; when she read about a Member of Parliament making a speech, she wanted to make that speech; when she read about how Lady Mary rode to hounds, teasing her sister-in-law and surprising everyone with her courage, she wanted to do it herself. But there was nothing to do, and so, fingering the smooth knife with her small hands, she forced herself to read."[11]

Emma Bovary devours books and imagines that the fictional lives are her own, that she is a heroine of Balzac or Sue. Don Quixote devours books and models his behavior according to certain fictional codes that he deems just and proper, though he knows that he himself is neither Lancelot nor Amadis. Anna Karenina sees in the fiction she reads neither ideal characters nor ideals of conduct, simply imaginary lives that taunt her with the life she herself is not living. Not the fictional life but her own life, not that of a Lady Mary but that of Anna Karenina, not as much an image of the world as an example of action in the world, an example of what it is like to live, while remaining aware that the life read is not her own. And just as Anna Karenina understands what it means to be Lady Mary without believing herself to be Lady Mary, we understand what it means to be Anna Karenina without ourselves being Anna Karenina. Without this understanding, fiction (and society itself) would be impossible. Or as Nicholas de Herberay would say, "Be with the style content / And ask not if what takes place is true."

"Literary characters are quicksand," wrote Blakey Vermeule in a fascinating study. "They are telescopes. They mire us down; they give us perspective." But "what happens," Vermeule asks, "when people get overly focused on the orienteering devices themselves, on the map rather than the road, on the telescope rather than the distant planet?" As Socrates put it to the hapless rhapsode Ion in Plato's dialogue, "What does it mean to be more interested in a representation of something than in the thing itself?" Vermeule notes that "Ion, of course, had no answer."[12]

And yet, perhaps an answer is possible. Perhaps Socrates's question to Ion (as Plato no doubt knew) is answered in that moment known to every true reader, in which a verse, a line of prose, an idea or a story, suddenly touches us, unexpectedly and profoundly, revealing something dark, half-intuited, unavowed, something that belongs exclusively to that reader to whom it has been secretly destined. That verse, sentence, or story will always interest us more than the material thing itself, because we are creatures of feeble perceptions, like moles in the sun, betrayed by our senses, and even though literary language is an uncertain, unreliable instrument, it is, however, capable, in a few miraculous moments, of helping us see the world.

The protagonists of Don Quixote's chivalric romances and of Emma Bovary's novels may be faint shadows of the real thing, but they are nevertheless powerful enough to overwhelm their readers—totally in the case of Emma, ambiguously in the case of Alonso Quijano—and compel them to tilt at windmills and inhabit romantic castles. Or, as in the case of Anna Karenina, to follow Flaubert's advice and "live." Even if death comes at the end.

Like Cervantes, Flaubert intuited this essential power of fiction, its extraordinary capacity to recreate and transmit our experience of "the thing itself." He knew also that we learn the tenets of our behavior not necessarily through material action but rather through stories in which this behavior is played out, with its various possible causes and consequences. On the stage set by the text, we see our own selves perform under a multitude of guises, and we can, and often do, learn something from what we see. Fiction is in this sense exemplary, and if the seeming infinity of plots does not exhaust the possibilities of our dealings with the world, some part of it, a certain episode or character, a particular detail in a story, will perhaps illuminate for us a turning point in our lives. Chesterton noted that "somewhere embedded in every ordinary book are five or six words for which really all the rest will be written":[13] it is in those five or six words that readers consciously or unconsciously seek to understand something of their own circumstances.

The meanings lent to the metaphors of the reader—as traveler, as resident of the ivory tower, as devourer of books—never remain the same for long. The bookworm changes its meaning from the gluttonous reader of the Anglo-Saxon riddle to the

obedient word eater of Revelation, from the wishful Emma to
the wishing Anna. Being a bookworm need not always carry a
negative connotation. We are reading creatures, we ingest words,
we are made of words, we know that words are our means of
being in the world, and it is through words that we identify our
reality and by means of words that we are ourselves identified.

NOTES

When the translator of a quotation is not mentioned, the translation is my own.

As I lack university training, my reading habits are less rigorous than those of academics, and often, when giving a source, I do not mention the page on which I found the original quotation. I hope the reader will forgive this fault, due less to carelessness than to an amateur's enthusiasm.

INTRODUCTION

Epigraph. Friedrich Nietzsche, *Posthumous Papers*.

1. See Aristotle, *The Art of Rhetoric*, IX:3:10, translated with an introduction and notes by H. C. Lawson-Tancred (Harmondsworth: Penguin, 1991), pp. 235–36.

2. Cicero, *Orator*, XXIII:78, translated by Albert Yon (Paris: Les Belles Lettres, 2002).

CHAPTER 1. THE READER AS TRAVELER

1. *Heures de Rohan à l'usage de Paris*, Ms 9471, Bibliothèque nationale de France, Paris.

2. See Louis Ginzberg, *The Legends of the Jews*, vol. 2, translated by Henrietta Szold (Baltimore: Johns Hopkins University Press, 1998), pp. 261–65.

3. Quoted in Dominique Charpin, *Lire et écrire à Babylone* (Paris: Presses Universitaires de France, 2008), pp. 18, 33, and 208.

4. Plotin, *Traités 1-6*, translated under the direction of Luc Brisson and Jean-François Pradeau, Traité III: 6, 20, p. 157 (Paris: Flammarion, 2002).

5. Sir Thomas Browne, *Religio Medici*, in *The Major Works*, edited with an introduction and notes by C. A. Patrides (Harmondsworth: Penguin Books, 1977).

6. See A. Gros, *Le thème de la route dans la Bible* (Brussels: La pensée catholique, 1957).

7. The word "road" appears more than six hundred times in the Old Testament. See Gros, *Le thème de la route dans la Bible*.

8. See I. A. Richards, *Principles of Literary Criticism* (London: Kegan Paul, 1924).

9. Habakkuk 2:2. Biblical quotations are taken from the King James Version.

10. Ezekiel 2:9.

11. Revelation 10:9–11.

12. See Ginzberg, *The Legends of the Jews*, vol. 3, translated by Paul Radin.

13. Quoted in Eusebius, *Preparation for the Gospel*, I:9:24, translated by Edwin Hamilton (Piscataway, N.J.: Gifford, Gorgias Press, 1903).

14. Saint Bonaventure, *Breviloquium*, II:11, in *The Works of Bonaventure*, vol. 2, translated from the Latin by José de Vinck (Paterson, N.J.: St. Anthony Guild Press, 1963).

15. Genesis 3:5.

16. See S. de Dietrich, *Le dessin de Dieu, itinèraire biblique* (Paris: Denachaux et Niestlé, 1948).

17. Saint Augustine, *Confessions*, I:13, p. 34.

18. Saint Augustine, *Confessions*, I:13, p. 33.

19. Yehuda Amichai, *Début fin début*, (Paris: Editions de l'éclat, 2001).

20. See Jean-Pierre Sonnet, *Le chant des montées: marcher à Bible ouverte* (Paris: Desclée de Brouwer, 2007).

21. See Saint Anthanasius, *The Life of St. Antony*, translated by R. T. Meyer (Mahwah, N.J.: Paulist Press, 1950), p. 56.

22. See Francis I Andersen, "Amos," in Bruce M. Metzger and Michael D. Coogan (eds.), *The Oxford Guide to People and Places in the Bible* (Oxford: Oxford University Press, 2001), p. 9.

23. John Bunyan, *The Pilgrim's Progress*, edited by Roger Sharrock (Harmondsworth: Penguin, 1965), p. 39.

24. Saint Augustine, *The Confessions*, XI:28, translated with an introduction by R. S. Pine-Coffin (Harmondsworth: Penguin, 1961).

25. The first tablet lacked half a column of text; only in 1975, thanks to a fragment discovered in Nippur, was the full text made available to us. See *L'Epopée de Gilgamesh: Le grand homme qui ne voulait pas mourir*, translated from the Akkadian and edited by Jean Bottéro (Paris: Gallimard, 1992).

26. *L'Epopée de Gilgamesh.*

27. See Jean-Jacques Glassner, *La Tour de Babylone: Que reste-t-il de la Mésopotamie?* (Paris: Editions du Seuil, 2003).

28. Quoted in Jesper Eidem and Jørgen Læssøe, *The Shemshara Archives, Volume 1: The Letters*, 23 (Copenhagen: Kongelige Danske videnskabernes selskab, 2001).

29. Herbert Mason, *Gilgamesh: A Verse Narrative*, with an afterword by John H. Marks (New York: New American Library, 1972).

30. Dante Alighieri, *Commedia, Inferno* I:7.

31. Dante, *Commedia, Inferno* I:91.

32. Titus Burckhardt, "Le Retour d'Ulysse," *Etudes Traditionnelles* (January–March 1979).

33. Dante Alighieri, *Commedia, Paradiso* II:1-6.

34. See E. R. Curtius, *Europäische Literatur und Lateinisches Mittelalter*, 11th edition (Tübingen: Francke, 1948).

35. This is, by and large, the poetic context from which Dante draws his sailing images, but he draws also, perhaps principally, from Cassien's *Collationes*, which, as Curtius points out, was very much read throughout the Middle Ages. See Curtius, *Europäische Literatur und Lateinisches Mittelalter*.

36. *Studi sulla Divina Commedia di Galileo Galilei, Vincenzo Borghini ed altri*, edited by Ottavio Gigli (Florence: Felice Le Monnier, 1855), pp. v–xiv.

37. Dante, *Commedia, Purgatorio* XXVII:142.

38. Dante, *Commedia, Paradiso* XXXIII:91.

39. Dante, *Commedia, Paradiso* XXXIII:85-87.

40. Dante, *Commedia, Paradiso* XXXIII:106-108.

41. See Sandro Botticelli, *The Drawings for Dante's Divine Comedy*, published on the occasion of the exhibition at the Royal Academy of Arts, London, 17 March–10 June 2001 (London: Royal Academy Publications, 2000).

42. John Barton and John Muddiman, editors of *The Oxford Bible Commentary* (Oxford: Oxford University Press, 2001), reject such an interpretation. "But no explanation is given in the text of God's preference, and it is not probable that the story, at any rate

in its present form, reflects an age-old rivalry between pastoralists and farmers."

43. Dante compares his enterprise to that which "threw Neptune in amazement at Argo's shadow" (Jason's ship). *Commedia, Paradiso* XXXIII:96.

44. Dante, *Commedia, Inferno* XXVI:125.

45. See George K. Anderson, *The Legend of the Wandering Jew* (Hanover, N.H.: Brown University Press, 1965).

46. R. Naz, "Pèlerinage," in Lefebvre, *Dictionnaire du droit canonique*, vol. VI (Paris, 1957).

47. Saint Augustine, *Sermon 141, 4, "Jesus notre route,"* in Raulx (ed.), *Oeuvres complètes de Saint Augustin* (Paris, 1838).

48. Saint Augustine, *Sermon 36, 413, "Corpus Christanorum."*

49. Dante, *Commedia, Inferno* I:30.

50. Dante, *Commedia, Paradiso* XIII:112–13.

51. Jurij M. Lotman, "Il viaggio di Ulisse nella *Divina Commedia* di Dante," in *Testo e contesto: Semiotica dell'arte e della cultura* (Bari: Laterza, 1980).

52. Dante Alighieri, *La vita nuova* XL, in *Vita nuova: Rime*, ed. Fredi Chiappelli (Milan: Murcia, 1965).

53. Dante, *Il Convivio* I:3:4.

54. Saint Augustine, *De Doctrina Christiana*, I:17.1–2. Quoted in Brian Stock, *Augustine the Reader: Meditation, Self-Knowledge, and the Ethics of Interpretation* (Cambridge, Mass.: Belknap Press of Harvard University Press, 1996).

55. Saint Augustine, *Confessions*, XI:2, p. 255.

56. Saint Bonaventure, "Itinerarium Mentis in Deo," in *The Works*

of Bonaventure, Volume I: Mystical Opuscula, translated from the Latin by José de Vinck (Paterson, N.J.: St. Anthony Guild Press, 1960), p. 58.

57. Dante, *Commedia, Paradiso* XXXIII:121–23.

58. Orhan Pamuk, *Silent House*, translated by Robert Finn (New York: Knopf, 2012), p. 334.

59. Cees Nooteboom, *Nomad's Hotel: Travels in Time and Space*, translated by Ann Kelland (London: Harvill Press and Secker, 2006), p. 1.

60. Cees Nooteboom, *Roads to Santiago: Detours and Riddles in the Lands & History of Spain*, translated by Ina Rilke (London: Harvill Press, 1997).

61. Petrarch, *Rerum familarum libri*, XV:5.

62. Nooteboom, *Nomad's Hotel*, p. 2.

63. Nooteboom, *Nomad's Hotel*, p. 7.

64. E. M. Forster, *Howards End*, chap. 22.

65. Nooteboom, *Nomad's Hotel*, p. 4.

66. Dante Alighieri, *Commedia, A Digital Edition*, edited by Prue Shaw, Scholarly Digital Editions, 2011, www.sd-editions.com/Commedia/index.html.

67. Jean Sarzana with Alain Pierrot, *Impressions numériques*, www.publie.net, published online 30 October 2010.

68. Dante, *Commedia, Inferno* XXVI:116.

69. Robert Louis Stevenson, *Travels with a Donkey in the Cevennes* (1879; New York: Scribner's, 1912), p. 63.

CHAPTER 2. THE READER IN THE IVORY TOWER

1. See Jos Koldeweij, Paul Vandenbroeck, and Bernard Vermet, *Hieronymus Bosch: The Complete Paintings and Drawings* (Rotterdam: NAi Publishers, 2001), p. 170.

2. Irving L. Zupnick, "Bosch's Representation of Acedia" in *Bosch in Prespective*, edited by James Snyder (Englewood Cliffs, N.J.: Prentice-Hall, 1973), p. 134.

3. Thomas Aquinas, in *Summa theologiae* 2:2, 179–81, discusses the distinction between the contemplative and the active lives, etymologically associating the former with rest and the latter with movement. "Therefore, because some men tend chiefly to contemplation of truth and others to exterior actions, the life of man is fittingly distinguished into active and contemplative" (Thomas Aquinas, *Selected Writings*, edited and translated by Ralph McInerny [Harmondsworth: Penguin, 1998], p. 684). Though in themselves both are good lives (in anagogical terms, Rachel represents the contemplative and Leah the active life), either can be perverted into sinful behavior stemming from insufficient love in the first case (leading to wrath and violence) and from excess of love in the second (leading to sloth or acedia).

4. Pseudo-Hippocrates, *Sur le rire et la folie* (Paris: Rivages, 1989).

5. Donald Attwater, *A Dictionary of Saints* (Harmondsworth: Penguin, 1965).

6. Saint Jerome, "Letter to Eustochium on Guarding Virginity," in *The Collected Works of Erasmus*, vol. 61, *Patristic Scholarship: The Edition of St. Jerome*, edited, translated, and annotated by James F. Brady and John. C. Olin (Toronto: University of Toronto Press, 1992).

7. Among others, see Raymond Klibansky, Erwin Panofsky, and Fritz Saxl, *Saturn and Melancholia* (London, 1964; rev. 1989); Anne Larue, *L'autre mélancholie: Acedia, ou les chambres de l'esprit* (Paris: Hermann, 2001); Jennifer Radden (ed.), *The Nature of Melancholy: From Aristotle to Kristeva* (Oxford: Oxford University Press, 2000).

8. Johann Wolfgang von Goethe, *Faust: Der Tragödie erster Teil*, "Nacht," in *Werke*, vol. III, Hamburg edition, edited by Erich Trunz (Munich: C. K. Beck, 1996).

9. Marcelo Ficino, "On Caring for the Health of the Man of Letters," in *Book of Life*, translated and with a new introduction by Charles Boer (Woodstock, Conn.: Spring Publications, 1980).

10. Quoted by Ficino, "On Caring for the Health of the Man of Letters," in *Book of Life*.

11. Ficino, "On Caring for the Health of the Man of Letters," in *Book of Life*.

12. Marcelo Ficino, "On Prolonging the Life of Scholars" in *Book of Life*.

13. Michel de Montaigne, "On Three Kinds of Social Intercourse," in *The Complete Essays*, translated and edited by M. A. Screech (Harmondsworth: Penguin, 1991), p. 933.

14. Peter Handke, *Ich bin Ein Bewohner des Elfenbeinturms: Aufsätze* (Frankfurt am Main: Suhrkamp, 1972), pp. 23, 32.

15. Henry James used the term as the title for one of the two novels left unfinished at his death in 1916 and published one year later (Henry James, *The Ivory Tower* [New York: Charles Scribner's Sons, 1917]).

16. Charles Auguste Sainte-Beuve, "Pensées d'août, à M. Villemain," "Et Vigny, plus secret, / Comme en sa tour d'ivoire, avant midi rentrait."

17. Proverbs 18:10.

18. Psalms 61:3.

19. Isaiah 2:15.

20. Song of Solomon 4:4 and 8:10.

21. Seneca, "De tranquillitate," in *Moral Essays*, ed. R. M. Gummere (Cambridge, Mass.: Harvard University Press, 1955).

22. John Carey, *The Intellectuals and the Masses: Pride and Prejudice Among the Literary Intelligensia, 1880–1939* (London: Faber and Faber, 1992).

23. George Moore, *Confessions of a Young Man, 1886: Edited and Annotated by George Moore, 1904 and Again in 1916* (Harmondsworth: Penguin, 1918).

24. William Shakespeare, *Hamlet*, V:2.

25. A. C. Bradley, *Shakespearean Tragedy* (New York: Macmillan/St. Martin's Press, 1966; rpt. Echo Library, 2006), p. 44.

26. Bradley, *Shakespearean Tragedy*, p. 62.

27. *Hamlet*, II:2.

28. *Hamlet*, III:1.

29. *Hamlet*, I:5.

30. John Gielgud, *Acting Shakespeare* (London: Pan Books, 1997).

31. *Hamlet*, I:2.

32. *Hamlet*, II:2.

33. William Shakespeare, *The Tempest*, III:2.

34. Stephen Greenblatt, *Will in the World: How Shakespeare Became Shakespeare* (New York: W.W. Norton, 2004).

35. William Shakespeare, *Love's Labour's Lost*, IV:2.

36. *Hamlet*, V:1.

37. Northrop Frye, *Northrop Frye on Shakespeare* (Markham, Ont.: Fitzhenry and Whiteside, 1986).

38. Thomas Aquinas, "Commendation of and Division of Sacred Scripture" (1256), in *Selected Writings*, edited and translated with

an Introduction and Notes by Ralph McInerny, (Harmondsworth: Penguin, 1998).

39. See Brian Stock, *Augustine the Reader: Meditation, Self-Knowledge, and the Ethics of Interpretation* (Cambridge, Mass.: Belknap Press of Harvard University Press, 1996).

40. *Hamlet*, II:2.

41. Samuel Taylor Coleridge, *Lectures and Notes on Shakspere [sic] and Other English Poets* (London: George Bell and Sons, 1904), pp. 368, 344.

42. *Hamlet*, I:5.

43. Virgil, *Aeneid*, VI:5, line 714.

44. *Hamlet*, II:2.

45. *Hamlet*, I:5.

46. Tom Stoppard, *Rosencrantz and Guildenstern Are Dead*, act I (New York: Grove Press, 1967).

47. Greenblatt, *Will in the World*.

48. Hastings Rashdall, *The Universities of Europe in the Middle Ages*, three vols., vol. II, chap. 12, sec. 3 (Oxford: Clarendon Press, 1985).

49. *Hamlet*, I:2.

50. Jonathan Bate, *Soul of the Age: A Biography of the Mind of William Shakespeare* (New York: Random House, 2009).

51. A. D. Nuttall, *Shakespeare the Thinker* (New Haven: Yale University Press, 2007).

52. Quoted in Onno van Wilgenburg, *The Play's the Thing: (Anti-)Nazi Shakespeare Appropriation 1933–1999*.

53. David Forgacs (editor), "Socialism and Culture," in *An Antonio Gramsci Reader: Selected Writings 1916–1935* (New York: Schocken Books, 1988).

54. Antonio Gramsci, *Prison Notebooks*, Vol. III, edited and translated by Joseph A. Buttigieg (New York: Columbia University Press, 2007).

55. Gramsci, *Prison Notebooks*, 2 vols., edited by Quentin Hoare and Geoffrey Nowell Smith (New York: Columbia University Press, 1996), vol. I.

56. C. L. R. James, "Notes on Hamlet," in *The C. L. R. James Reader*, edited and introduced by Anna Grimshaw (Oxford: Blackwell, 1992).

57. Franz Kafka, "Jeder Mensch trägt ein Zimmer in sich," from "Oktavheft 2," in *Oxforder Octavhefte 1 & 2: Historisch-Kritische Ausgabe sämtlicher Handschriften, Drucke und Typoskripte,*edited by Roland Reuß and Peter Staengle (Frankfurt am Main: Stroemfeld/ Roter Stern, 2006), p. 35.

58. Nicholas Carr, *The Shallows: What the Internet Is Doing to Our Brains* (New York: W. W. Norton, 2010).

CHAPTER 3. THE BOOKWORM

1. "Bening lecteur, de jugement pourveu, / Quand tu verras l'invention gentille / De cest autheur: contente toy du stille, / Sans t'enquerir s'il est vray ce, qu'as leu." Nicholas de Herberay, Seigneur des Essars, "Au lecteur, sonnet de Herberay," in *Soleil du soleil: Anthologie du sonnet français* (Paris: Gallimard, 2000).

2. Umberto Eco, *The Limits of Interpretation* (Bloomington: Indiana University Press, 1990).

3. See Bruno Bettelheim, *The Uses of Enchantment: The Meaning and Importance of Fairy Tales* (New York: Vintage, 1989).

4. Desiderius Erasmus, *In Praise of Folly*.

5. William Blades, *The Enemies of Books*, second edition revised and enlarged by the author (London: Elliot Stock, 1888). Blades notes that "Hooke is evidently describing the 'Lepsima.'" Among the book-eating pests, Blade lists not only several varieties of *Anobium* but also the horny-headed and strong-jawed *Oecophora pseudospretella*.

6. *A Choice of Anglo-Saxon Verse*, selected, with an introduction and a parallel verse translation by Richard Hamer (London: Faber and Faber, 1970), pp. 106–7.

7. 1 Corinthians 3:18–19. "18: Let no man deceive himself. If any man among you seemeth to be wise in this world, let him become a fool, that he may be wise. 19: For the wisdom of this world is foolishness with God."

8. Boethius, *The Consolation of Philosophy*, translated by David R. Slavitt (Cambridge, Mass.: Harvard University Press, 2008).

9. Boethius, *The Consolation of Philosophy*, translated into English prose and verse by H. R. James (London: Elliot Stock, 1897).

10. Ezekiel 2:9–10.

11. Revelation 10:9–11.

12. See Virginie Poels, "Sarkozy et la Princesse de Clèves," *Marianne2*, Paris, 17 February 2009.

13. Hélène Cixous, "Nicolas Sarkozy, the Murderer of the Princesse de Clèves," *Guardian*, London, 23 March 2011.

14. Michel Pastoureau, "La Symbolique médiévale du livre," in *La Symbolique du livre dans l'art occidental du haut Moyen Age à Rembrandt* (Bordeaux: Société des Bibliophiles de Guyenne, and Paris: Institut d'étude du livre, 1995).

15. See, for example, the Bestiary of Pierre de Beauvais (thirteenth

century) in *Bestiaires du Moyen Age, mis en français moderne et présentés par Gabriel Bianciotto* (Paris: Stock, 1980).

16. Platón, "Carta séptima" in *Protágoras, Gorgias, Carta séptima*, p. 285, translated and with a preface by Javier Martínez García (Madrid: Alianza, 1998).

17. Sem Tob de Carrión, *Proverbos morales*, vv. 460–64, ed. I. González Llubera (Cambridge: Cambridge University Press, 1947).

18. Joannot Martorell and Martí Joan de Galba, *Tirant lo Blanc* (1490), translated by David H. Rosenthal (New York: Schocken Books, 1984), xxix.

19. Miguel de Cervantes, *Don Quijote de la Mancha*, vol. I, chap. VI, p. 49, edited and with notes by Celina S. de Cortázar and Isaías Lerner (Buenos Aires: Editorial Universitaria de Buenos Aires, 1969).

CONCLUSION. READING TO LIVE

1. Gustave Flaubert, letter to Mlle. Leroyer de Chantepie, 6 June 1857, in *Correspondance*, selected and edited by Bernard Masson (Paris: Gallimard, 1979), p. 343. Flaubert is advising his friend to read Montaigne, but I believe the advice is valid in a much more general sense.

2. "Quand le peuple ne croira plus à l'Immaculée Conception, il croira aux tables tournantes. Il faut se consoler de cela et vivre dans une tour d'ivoire. Ce n'est pas gai, je le sais; mais avec cette méthode, on n'est ni dupe ni charlatan." In *Correspondance*.

3. Gustave Flaubert, "Le Bibliomane." "Il aimait un livre, parce que c'était un livre; il aimait son odeur, sa forme, son titre. Ce qu'il aimait dans un manuscrit, c'était sa vieille date illisible, les lettres gothiques, bizarres et étranges, les lourdes dorures qui chargeaient les dessins;

c'étaient ces pages couvertes de poussière, poussière dont il aspirait avec délice le parfum suave et tendre. C'était ce joli mot *finis*, entouré de deux amours, portés sur un ruban, s'appuyant sur une fontaine, gravé sur une tombe, ou reposant dans une corbeille, entre les roses et les pommes d'or et les bouquets bleus. // Cette passion l'avait absorbé tout entier: il mangeait à peine, il ne dormait plus; mais il rêvait des jours et des nuits entières à son idée fixe, les livres. Il rêvait à tout ce que devait avoir de divin, de sublime et de beau, une bibliothèque royale, et il rêvait à s'en faire une aussi grande que celle d'un roi. Comme il respirait à son aise, comme il était fier et puissant lorsqu'il plongeait sa vue dans les immenses galeries où son oeil se perdait dans les livres! Il levait la tête, des livres—il l'abaissait, des livres—à droite, à gauche, encore des livres. // Il savait à peine lire."

4. Gustave Flaubert, letter to Louise Colet, Saturday, 12 June 1852 (19 June in the Pléiade edition): "Je retrouve toutes mes origines dans le livre que je savais par coeur avant de savoir lire, *Don Quichotte,* et il y a de plus, par dessus, l'écume agitée des mers normandes, la maladie anglaise, le brouillard puant." In *Correspondance.*

5. Gustave Flaubert, letter to Louise Colet, 22 November 1852: "Ce qu'il y a de prodigieux dans Don Quichotte, c'est l'absence d'art et cette perpétuelle fusion de l'illusion et de la réalité qui en fait un livre si comique et si poétique. Quels nains que tous les autres à côté! Comme on se sent petit, mon Dieu! comme on se sent petit!" In *Correspondance.*

6. Gustave Flaubert, letter to Guy de Maupassant, Croiset, 4 May 1880: "L'importance attachée à des niaiseries, le pédantisme de la futilité m'exaspèrent! Bafouns le chic!" In *Correspondance.*

7. Gustave Flaubert, *Madame Bovary*: "Ce qui le séduisait par-dessus tout, c'était le chic."

8. Flaubert, *Madame Bovary*, chap. IX: "Elle lut Balzac et George Sand, y cherchant des assouvissements imaginaires pour ses convoitises personnelles."

9. A. S. Byatt, "Scenes from a Provincial Life," *The Guardian*, 27 July 2002.

10. Charlotte Lennox, *The Female Quixote or The Adventures of Arabella* (1752) (London: Pandora Press, 1986).

11. Leo Tolstoy, *Anna Karenina*, translated by Richard Pevear and Larissa Volokhonsky (New York: Viking Penguin, 2001).

12. Blakey Vermeule, *Why Do We Care About Literary Characters?* (Baltimore: Johns Hopkins University Press, 2010), pp. 246–47.

13. G. K. Chesterton, "Dombey and Son," in *Chesterton on Dickens*, Introduction by Michael Slater (London: J. M. Dent and Sons, 1992).

INDEX

ACKNOWLEDGMENTS

Thanks to David McKnight and the board of the University of Pennsylvania for asking me to deliver the Rosenbach Lectures, which led me to write this book. Thanks to the several librarians at the Free Library, the Rosenbach Library, the University of Pennsylvania Library, and the Jewish Center Library of Philadelphia for their hospitality and generosity during my visit. Special thanks to Fr. Lucien-Jean Bord, chief librarian at the Abbey of Saint-Martin in Ligugé, who generously guided me through the stacks and helped me with many essential suggestions. Above all, thanks to Jerry Singerman, who, with intelligence, erudition, and kindness, proved my prejudices against editors shamefully wrong.

www.ingramcontent.com/pod-product-compliance
Ingram Content Group UK Ltd.
Pitfield, Milton Keynes, MK11 3LW, UK
UKHW040823090225
454781UK00002B/51/J